THE LAST SAILORS

THE LAST SAILORS
THE FINAL DAYS OF WORKING SAIL

NEIL HOLLANDER AND HARALD MERTES

St. Martin's Press   New York

Design by Kingsley Parker

Library of Congress Cataloging in Publication Data

Hollander, Neil.
    The last sailors.

    1. Sailboats.   2. Work boats.   3. Seafaring life.
I. Mertes, Harald.   II. Title.
VM321.H58   1984   623.8′ 2026   83–19101
ISBN 0–312–47139–4

First Edition
10 9 8 7 6 5 4 3 2 1

"Les marins, vois-tu, ne ressemblent pas au reste du monde."
—Renan

CONTENTS

FOREWORD

Here you will find the true saga of sail—largely unfamiliar and overlooked. This book is not about sailors who man the helm for speed and efficiency, nor is it another account of one man's spectacular voyage. It is rather a look at what remains of the most ancient form of movement of wind on water.

The sails of today are made to win races, or perhaps to give a few city-weary executives an afternoon of fun. We have forgotten the history of wind and sail, where the simplest of crafts have ventured out beyond the horizon in search of new lands.

Forty years ago, I sailed with some of the most heroic of these men on log rafts called *jangadas*. We traveled from the northeast of Brazil all the way down to Rio. That voyage was an attempt to protest the terrible poverty of these men. My own experience with the *jangadieros* has now been shared by the authors of this book, and they have gone on to find other mariners throughout the world who—whether fishing or trading—still maintain their own particular and very ancient nautical customs.

It is cause for rejoicing that some record of these wonderful "old men of the sea" has been preserved within these pages.

—Orson Welles

INTRODUCTION:

MAN AND CRAFT

Times are changing rapidly for the deep-water sailor who hoists sail and sets out to gain his livelihood from the sea. He is being left in the wake of technology. We wanted to record the final days of working sail and to do this we decided to crew on board junks, trading schooners, barges, and other working sailboats.

Of course, it is the men who are disappearing. Many of the boats remain: artifacts, harbored ashore in museums. But it is difficult to preserve the sailor's eternal triangle—man, boat, and sea. This unique and delicate balance of man against the elements forms the working sailor's way of life: his duties, his hardships and pleasures, his folklore, and his ties to his family and the shore.

We found that very little has been written about them. Tall ships, record-breaking voyages, and yachting adventures have been the popular sailing subjects. Aside from several anthropological studies and the occasional article, there have been few attempts to document what remains of working sail.

We began to search systematically for those places in the world where sailing craft are still part of the economic system. We corresponded with diplomats, harbor-masters, commercial travelers, and yachtsmen cruising abroad, asking each what he had seen of working sail. All too often the replies were "Sorry, you're five years too late," or "The last one is now in a museum." In spite of frequent disappointments, we finally prepared a list of countries where traditional sailing craft can still be found. We could not, of course, visit each place. Instead we made a selection and the result is a sample of the world's working sail:

the Windward Islands schooner
the Brazilian *jangada*
the Chilean *lancha chilota*
the Egyptian *aiyassa*
the Sri Lankan *oruwa*
the Bangladeshi *shampan*
the Chinese junk
the Indonesian *pinisi*

We have chosen these craft on the basis of geographic and cultural diversity, the type of craft, and the kind of work in which each is engaged: fishing, trading, or transporting cargo and passengers. Some of these craft are already obsolete, and the rest will undoubtedly soon follow.

Commercial sail will continue to exist, and—given the current energy crisis—even thrive, but the form will have changed radically. Giant sheets of aluminum will be winched into place by electric motors, then reefed and trimmed by commands from a computer. A new type of sailor will be at the helm, more a technician than a deck-hand and more often in front of a control panel than in the bows facing the seas. The long era of traditional sail is rapidly drawing to a close and its end is our present.

The beginnings of sail are lost in a primeval mist, but more than likely the first sailors set out on board tree trunks. The first sail was probably nothing more elaborate than a leafy branch held aloft to catch the wind. There was only one course, downwind, but sailors soon learned that the more branches they held or lashed on, the faster their logs would go.

Strangely enough, this first sail, the branch, remained in use until just a few decades ago. On the northern coast of Haiti, natives used a simple raft of four or five logs to carry fruit along the coast to market. It was called a *pri-pri*, the Creole equivalent of *petit prix;* after the fruit was sold the raft was sold as well, but for a small price since it could not make the return trip upwind.

The sailing raft is certainly one of man's original craft and has had its own distinctive evolution. At one time rafts of bamboo and balsa could be found on almost every continent, and generations of sailors have set out to sea with little more than a few logs bound together with dowels or lashings. In some places in the world, most notably Peru, Formosa, and India, the rafts became highly sophisticated with tapered bows, deck houses, and multiple masts.

On the west coast of South America sailing rafts fashioned from balsa logs reached enormous proportions, far larger than those of Heyerdahl's famed *Kon Tiki.* These rafts sometimes used twenty or thirty logs for the float and were capable of carrying upward of seventy tons of cargo.

Above the raft were one or more decks, supported by a cribwork of logs, often three or four meters in height. The decks were used as living quarters for the crew, and the helmsman stood on the highest platform wielding a long steering oar.

Cumbersome, slow, and dangerous in a rough sea, these rafts made regular trips of up to a thousand miles until the eighteenth century. Like a *pri-pri* voyage, it was always a one-way trip; at their destination, both raft and cargo were sold.

Most of the world's sailing rafts exist now only as museum models, but in isolated villages in northeastern Brazil a survivor remains—the *jangada.* There is not a single piece of iron or steel used in its construction, and those *jangadas* that sail out to fish today are virtually identical to those built after the Portuguese arrived in the sixteenth century.

The dugout canoe reaches back almost unchanged into history. The first canoes were probably made from strips of bark, then later used as prototypes for those hewn from trees. Dugouts are still widely used on rivers and inland waters, but seagoing canoes under sail have become a much rarer species. They are the real ancestors of modern ships.

The Sri Lankan *oruwa* is a craft in transition, something more than just an outrigger canoe, but less than a planked ship. A dugout forms the bottom half of the hull, and the top half is made up of washboards that are sewn to the gunwales for protection against the waves. The idea of a planked hull is incipient, while at the same time the form of the traditional craft is maintained. Should a larger craft be needed, a second set of washboards could be added, then a third, and so on. The boat could grow and the dugout at its base would slowly be transformed into a keel.

There are two great maritime traditions—Western and Eastern—and until comparatively recently there was little contact between the two. According to legend the origin of all Chinese craft is the humble *sampan*—"three planks," one for the bottom and two for the sides.

This basic *sampan* has dozens of variations, many of which now sail far beyond China. The Bangladeshi *shampan* is a typical export, a craft that over the years gradually adapted to a new nautical environment. The junk sails were replaced by a lateen rig and the bow shaped to a point, but the familiar palmiped form is still there, expanded so that the ship can transport bulk cargoes such as rice, salt, and coal. Fleets of *shampans* still ply the Gulf of Bengal, one of the last strongholds of traditional sail. Merchantmen, pirates, smugglers, and fishermen all share the same muddy waters and struggle to coexist.

The junk is also patterned after the *sampan,* and the junk's watertight compartments resemble individual *sampans* joined together to form a larger whole. In the thirteenth and fourteenth centuries, the Chinese built ships over 100 meters long, an engineering feat the West did not achieve until hundreds of years later. When the two maritime traditions did finally meet in full force, the Chinese empire had all but disappeared and Western clipper ships easily dominated the China Seas. The junks that sail today are mere quarter-size models of what they had once been. Now they simply follow the coast and seldom venture out of sight of land.

Unfortunately, there are no clipper ships still in trade. Sail has disappeared so rapidly that the best we could find to represent the Western tradition were the last remnants of a trading fleet. The Windward Islands schooners that still sail between the islands of the Caribbean are tramps, typically in bad repair, and forever shuttling from port to port in search of cargoes. Their crews are outcasts, men who cannot find work elsewhere, who would jump ship the moment they thought they could get a job ashore.

The Indonesian *pinisi,* also a schooner, is a mixture of the two traditions. The *pinisi's* hull is constructed in the Eastern fashion—the shell first and then the ribs—but its gaff rig is clearly of Western origin. More profitable than the Windward Islands schooner, hundreds of *pinisi* still crisscross the Java Sea hauling timber from Borneo and Sumatra to the markets of Java.

We decided to include two other craft, both drawn from what was probably the most numerous group of working sailboats, the lighters, barges, pilot cutters, ferries, and coasters that were once the backbone of commerce. Both boats, the Egyptian *aiyassa* and the Chilean *lancha chilota* (a barge and a timber sloop) are nearly the last of their kind, and neither has a long or distinguished pedigree. They are functional craft with few embellishments, whose rigs are simple enough to be operated by the customary crew, an old man and a boy. Each chapter in this book focuses on a different craft. There are only eight of them, a meager handful of the hundreds, if not thousands, of kinds of sailing boats that could once be found in the world's ports. Nonetheless, the boats represent various maritime traditions. The Brazilian sailing raft, the Sri Lankan outrigger canoe, and the Bangladeshi *shampan* all reach back toward the origins of man's relationship with the sea. The Chinese junk typifies the Eastern tradition, the Windward Islands schooner, the Western, and the Indonesian *pinisi*, the mixture of the two. The Egyptian sailing barge and the Chilean sloop are examples of the kind of smaller working craft that were once a common sight on the rivers and around the coasts of the world.

Our search lasted nearly two years, from 1981 to 1983. In each port and on board every boat we tried to meet the men who work these craft as fellow sailors interested in whatever they might be doing or thinking, and willing to take part if an extra hand was needed. Wherever possible, we have worked as crew and tried to share their way of life. Often we spent days, or even weeks, getting to know them, and letting them get to know us, before the cameras appeared.

We have tried to let the men speak for themselves of their lives afloat and ashore, working alongside them and meeting their families. Since between us we speak the major European languages we seldom needed a translator. When we did require one, it was always easy to find a local sailor who had voyaged abroad.

The end of this long tradition of working sail is a difficult one for those trying to maintain a livelihood. Ways of life are in conflict, and even the sea is not big enough to keep them all afloat.

THE LAST SAILORS

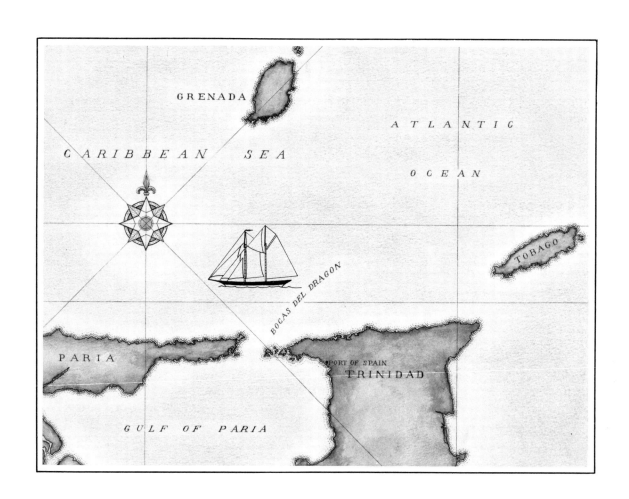

THE WINDWARD ISLANDS SCHOONER

Standing on the congested quay in Port of Spain, Trinidad, we watched the crew of the *Albert George* unload the cargo. Crates of green bananas passed from hand to hand out of the schooner's hold and onto the bed of a truck, and with them came an endless stream of banter and curses.

We found the Captain and the agent in the cab of the truck sorting out bills of lading. Both were surprised at our request.

"What!" exclaimed the agent. "You want to sail on that schooner!"

"I don't take passengers," said the Captain. "There aren't enough lifejackets."

"We'll go as crew, we're sailors."

"You're joking, of course," replied the agent.

"Not at all."

The Captain looked at us sceptically, trying to appraise our strength. "Are you willing to work?" he asked.

"What do you mean?"

"Load the cargo, set the sails, just like everyone else?"

"Yes, of course."

"I warn you, it won't be easy."

"We've done it before."

"All right," he said. "I'll sign you on."

The Captain of the Port and the Immigration Officer were amused to find our names at the bottom of the crew list, and after a few coarse jokes at our expense they stamped the document.

Tub, the mate, took charge of us and as soon as we stowed our gear below he assigned us places in the human chain unloading the cargo. The moment we stepped into the line, the boxes of bananas seemed to move faster and arrive in our hands charged with momentum. Before long, our biceps began to turn blue and each crate was another blackening blow. Our initiation to schooner life had begun.

The crew, we soon discovered, mirror their ship—rough, unkempt, their clothes patched like the sails, their origins as diverse as the schooner's ports of call. For that backbreaking task, heaving tons of merchandise from the quay to the hold and back again, they are paid less than a worker ashore, given a tiny cramped berth, and fed a monotonous diet of rice, yams, and beans, spliced only with whatever they can catch from the sea or pilfer from the cargo.

Why do sailors sign on? We asked many people that question. Jobs are scarce, they replied, especially for the unskilled, many men know no other way to live, and, as always, there are those who have their own, very private reasons for going to sea.

Four years earlier, we had arrived in Port of Spain from the other direction—the sea—and had a completely different impression of the schooners. After a two-week voyage from Brazil we sailed our small yacht through the islands of the Dragon's

Between the smaller islands, the schooner is still a ferry, a scheduled sailboat that is the cheapest way to travel.

Teeth and met a Windward Islands schooner drifting out with the tide and raising sail. Framed against Trinidad's green hills, she was a magnificent sight. Her long gaff boom slowly rose to the gallows, the Trade Wind filled her sails, then almost instantly her naked bow knifed through the water sending up clouds of spume. The Captain stood on the poop, shouting his orders, while forward the crew strained at the blocks.

We waved as we passed alongside, and suddenly both of us had the same *déjà vu*. We had seen it all before, if not in fact, then in old drawings and yellowed photographs—a proud windjammer sets her sails and leaps forward to meet the sea.

As we worked on deck shifting cargo, our arms becoming stiffer and stiffer, there were no fanciful pictures in our minds. The windjammer pride and polish, that legendary spirit that fills so many novels, was not to be found. Instead, the schooner reeked of neglect and decay. Her sails were worn and brown with mildew, her decks scarred, and her rigging rusted and makeshift. She is treated like a nautical boxcar, literally a vessel to be filled and emptied and shunted from port to port. Barely seaworthy and afloat by the grace of her pumps, the *Albert George* limps through the islands, crewed by a ragged collection of outcasts and drifters.

The mate, Tub, placidly watched us

struggle with the crates, our strength obviously dwindling, and if it amused him, he did not reveal it. Quick-tempered and the first to begin and end a brawl, he had earned his position on board by sheer strength, and he always saved the most difficult tasks for himself, such as throwing the boxes of bananas from the bottom of the hold onto the deck. His expression was nearly always the same, calm and immobile, yet he was ready to flash into anger the instant anyone challenged him. While standing watch or prowling with him through portside bars, we slowly got to know him better.

A stolen case of beer awaited us when the loading was finished and a second test of endurance began—a much more pleasurable one, however. After a while he came to realize that he had nothing to fear from us and that allowed him to express himself with more than just his fists.

He had always wanted to be a sailor, he told us. "As soon as the school bell rang I'd run down to the quay and wait for a schooner to sail in. Sometimes they'd throw me the line and I felt so good when I tied it around the bollard."

The three of us were sitting on the roof of the deckhouse, leaning against the gaff and boom and finishing the evening meal of rice and beans.

Tub thumped on the roof with his heel. Immediately, the cook peered over the edge. Tub threw the tin plates to him, ordered coffee, then rolled three cigarettes and passed them out.

"I was fourteen when I stowed away on the *Lazy Dolphin* for Barbados: boarded her at night, crawled into the hold and slept. We were out to sea before they saw me. The crew cuffed me about like I was a dog, the Captain the worst. He cursed and beat me with a piece of old rope so I couldn't walk. I screamed as he swore.

"When we tied up in Barbados, he sent me home on the first boat. The next time the *Lazy Dolphin* was in Saint George's a couple of weeks later, I stowed away again. All hell broke loose. Mad? Oh, my sweet Jesus, that Captain was so mad, seemed he'd have a stroke on the spot. He threw me this way and that way, beat me with that piece of old rope. I crawled into the stern and every time he turned and saw me there he'd let go of the wheel and come at me screaming, 'Are you going to stow away again?'

"No matter how loud I yelled and how much it hurt, I nodded 'yes.' At suppertime the cook gave me a bowl of soup and after the Captain had eaten he softened a bit, or maybe his arm just got tired. Anyway, he threw me his bowl and spoon and shouted, 'Get into the galley and start washing dishes.' "

Tub stared into his empty coffee mug. He didn't like to talk about his early years at sea. "Nigger days," he called them as he shut the door to his past.

"What happened to the *Lazy Dolphin?*" we asked.

"Went onto the rocks years ago. I got a job on another schooner. I've worked on lots of them, been sailing for more than ten years. This schooner is no better than the others. The whole crew, me included, would like to jump ship. Not to work on shore; no, not that, but to sign on an 'iron-boat,' you know, one of those island steamers. But it's not easy to get a berth. These days they're as rare as free drinks.

"I've had enough of schooners. They're all the same, slave ships, every one of

The hold is home for the crew, their berths, a pallet of cargo.

them. Work, sleep, work, that's all we do. Most of the time we're shifting cargo by hand—thirty tons of freight each trip.

"That was 1,000 cases of Heinekens you two dropped into the hold today and I caught and stacked them all. Tomorrow, when we get to Grenada, I'll have to throw every one of those bastards back on deck.

"Right now I'd like to go ashore and have a drink, just a beer or two before we sail, but I can't. I haven't got the money. I never seem to have any. I get paid, then one night, two nights later it's all gone. It's not my fault. Everybody has to live it up occasionally."

The three of us went ashore and just beyond the port gates we entered a stark, seedy street, the kind one finds on any waterfront. A collection of drunks and petty thieves cluttered the street corners and we gave them a wide berth. We headed for the nearest bar. Tub eyed the women standing in the doorways.

"A good sailor should have a woman in port, and I could too if I just had the money. Women are expensive these days, and you've either got to stop drinking or win at poker to afford one.

"It's only the Captain and the agent who don't have to worry in this business. They've got all the money. You should see their women, real uptown ladies, all fancy dressed like Christmas trees. Most of them won't even step on board this dirty boat. They wait in taxis.

"We'll be sailing tonight and it's easy to tell when—about ten minutes after the taxis arrive. The Captain will come on board talking soft and smelling like flowers. But that won't last long. Not tonight, anyway."

We stood in the open door of the bar fanned by an unusually cool breeze. Tub gestured toward the sky, which was rapidly becoming overcast.

"Wind's picking up fast," he said, "and it's going to be like the last trip when it blew all night. We were hauling on the sheets and lashing down the deck cargo. Then one of the blocks jammed and the Captain sent me aloft to clear it. I sat up there on the crosstrees, swinging from side to side like a drunk. It was so dark I couldn't even see the deck and I said to myself—'What the hell am I doing, risking my life for a couple of thousand cases of beer?' I'm still asking myself that question. And I'm not getting any answers either."

"But not every trip is like that, is it?" we said.

"No, but that doesn't make them any better. When we do have a moment or two to rest the Captain makes me sit by the wheel and listen to his stories. I've heard them every trip for years. I know them better than he does. I'll tell you what burns me the most. It's when we come into port, any port, and tie up next to one of those ironboats and see how those sailors live. We're jammed into the hold like cargo, but they've got private berths. And a real toilet. No buckets for them. That's the life—half the work, twice the pay, and plenty of women in the ports. One way or another, I'm going to get me a berth on an ironboat."

We sauntered back to the port and waiting for us on the quay was the last truckload of beer. Tub assembled the crew. Once again we took our places in the line and cases bounced from hand to hand into the hold. The pace was slower this time, nonetheless the edges of the crates cut deeply into our arms, which it seemed

would never have a chance to heal. Ten of us worked for nearly an hour to unload the truck, while less than 100 meters away a huge crane effortlessly moved pieces of machinery, each of which equaled the weight of our entire cargo.

How do schooners like the *Albert George* manage to exist?

"The present is still looking for them," explained an agent, "and will find them—soon."

The schooners have survived only because, until recently, the volume of trade in the southern Caribbean has been small, an insignificant trickle by international standards. The cargoes they have carried haven't been valuable enough to go by air, nor in sufficient quantities to fill a freighter's hold. Fruit and vegetables from the northern islands of Tobago, Grenada, and Saint Vincent were transported south to the markets of Trinidad, and general cargo to stock shops and bars paid for the return trip north. For a long while it seemed that the schooners had found a home in the economic system.

However, in recent years the trade has grown and a new challenge has appeared. Small coastal steamers, relics from the North Sea and the Baltic, are now gradually taking over the business. Too old and no longer economically viable in European waters, they are sold for little more than their scrap value and businessmen from the Caribbean are ready buyers.

Once again, history repeats itself—the propeller leaves sail in its wake. And no one voices any regret. Quite the contrary, the change is welcomed. A schooner Captain saves for the day he can fly to Europe and sail home in an ironboat. Sailors rush to work on board them. Wages are higher, living conditions less cramped, and most of the cargo is easily shifted by winch.

But the people who have irrevocably sealed the schooner's fate are the shipping agents, the kingpins of the trade, who prefer to send their cargoes in steel hulls. The rates may be slightly higher, but the loading and unloading is quicker and delivery dates are not subject to the whims of wind and sea.

The schooners now vie for the leftovers of the trade, freight, and passengers to the smallest of the islands, or those goods no one else wishes to transport such as building stone, cement, empty drums, and beer bottles. But even these "poor man's car-goes" will soon be taken away. Every year more ironboats arrive from Europe and the competition becomes keener. The schooners are slowly being squeezed out of the market, and eventually there will be nothing left on the quay for them to transport.

John, the owner and Captain of the *Fortress*, sat on the stern of his ironboat watching the two white links in the black chain strain to keep up with the pace. While we worked and sweated in the sun finishing the loading of the *Albert George*, he relaxed in the shade of an awning, sipping a Guinness, his feet propped up on the rail.

When the truck was empty and the

Georgetown, Grenada: part of the port still belongs to the schooners.

hatch closed, he waved us on board and offered us each a cold beer.

Wearing a white shirt, pressed pants, and sunglasses, John looked more like a businessman than a Captain. He ran the *Fortress* on a tight schedule, and handled his own accounts, which he kept neatly ordered in a filing cabinet in his cabin. He viewed the schooners with amusement and disdain, like the owner of a sleek motor cruiser who smirks when he passes a dugout canoe.

"Navigation isn't very difficult in the Caribbean," he said. "Most of the islands are so close together you are rarely out of sight of land. The only big patch of open water lies between here, Trinidad, and Grenada, one hundred twenty miles to the north. After that, if you keep sailing northward, there's an island every twenty miles or so all the way up the chain to Jamaica.

"To get lost, you really have to work at it. And that's fortunate, because most of those schooner captains can't navigate worth a damn. I know. I've wasted years on those boats. It may be hard to believe, but the truth of the matter is they don't know what they're doing. Just because they manage to get the schooner from A to B and back for ten years or so doesn't count for much. Going north or south the wind is on your beam. Just hoist the sail and away you go. That isn't very difficult."

"But they have a compass on board," we said. "We've seen them."

"Of course they do, and they look at it occasionally too. But so what? Does that mean they know how it works? Ask them. They'll tell you if you sail at ten you'll get to Grenada and one hundred ninety will bring you back. Maybe and maybe not. God only knows when it was last adjusted.

There is little lumber left in the islands. The masts and booms come from the jungles of South America.

They don't know what magnetism is. They haven't the slightest idea why that little needle always points north, or at least why it's supposed to point north. A good part of the time it doesn't.

"Those schooners make night passages, and since they have no electrics on board, they often rig a flashlight, a steel one, of course, just above the compass. That's usually enough to throw it off twenty or thirty degrees. I've seen them lash steel drums alongside the compass or stack oxygen cylinders next to it. Don't tell me they know what they're doing."

"But what if they get blown off course?" we asked.

"That happens sometimes. Then, the only thing they know how to do is remember in which direction they were blown and for how long, and then, when the storm is over, sail back to the place where they left their original course. That's not very imaginative, but if you don't know the basics and you can hardly add and subtract, what else can you do?

"In the old days when a schooner got lost, the Captain would throw a pig in the water. Supposedly, the animal would smell

land and start swimming toward it. That's not just some tale, they really did it. And don't laugh, because it often worked. You see, the pig would smell the molasses and sugar cane fields and start swimming toward his next meal. Clever, but you can hardly call that navigation.

"The strange thing is few boats get lost, or sink, and there aren't that many accidents either. Not as many as you might expect. There's something peculiar about those schooners. When trouble comes, no one can be luckier than they are. The day God passed out luck, those schooner captains were in the front of the line.

"Last Christmas one Captain bought his crew a case of rum, and naturally they drank it on the spot, tied up here at the dock. That's the boat over there," he said, pointing to a schooner painted a curious blend of pink and green and riding at anchor not far away.

"The whole lot of them sprawled on the deck drinking and singing until they fin-

ished off all twelve bottles. To this day no one knows who came up with the idea to sail to Tobago, but someone certainly did, because about midnight they cast off, raised sail, and headed for the *Bocas* ['mouths'—several narrow passages between the islands on the northwestern tip of Trinidad].

"They found them all right. The stupid, drunken bastards sailed straight into the first island, a good half mile off course. They hit the rocks, smashed a ruddy great hole in the starboard side, and by rights, she should have gone down. But she didn't. She just floated away. You see, the boat was loaded with empty gasoline drums. Try to explain that kind of luck!"

"It's easy," we said. "It's not luck, just a good story."

"No, I'm not putting you on."

We smiled. "You're not the first Captain we've talked to."

"I'm telling you the truth, although it may not sound like it. But some of the things that happen around here are so incredible no one could make them up. And a lot of them have nothing to do with luck either. There are a few schooner captains who can't afford to put their chips on fate. I'm not giving out any names. But you can find them if you really want to. They're the ones smuggling liquor and cigarettes, and if you want to survive in that business, you always have to know exactly where you are. A couple of miles off course can sail you straight into jail."

At first, John was hesitant to talk about the smuggling trade, but the subject is common knowledge, if seldom common conversation, and there is no secret about how the business operates.

Since many of the Caribbean islands have placed high tariffs on imported goods, particularly liquor and cigarettes, smuggling flourishes as perhaps never before and the profits can be enormous. A clever Captain with a fast boat and a little luck can make a fortune. At one time or another many of the schooners have "made the trip north," as sailors call the voyage.

In "the north" are islands like Saint Barts, where liquor and cigarettes can be purchased at duty-free prices, and payment made in nearly any currency. Questions are rarely asked as a schooner fills its hold with contraband or *bobol.*

Once the boat arrives in "the south," a lonely bay, unpatrolled by customs agents, is usually not hard to find.

"There are still quite a few smugglers left," John continued, "especially with today's prices. I really don't know how many, perhaps ten, fifteen boats around here. That's just a guess. It's a risky business. Get caught once, and you lose your boat."

He spun a yarn about a schooner that was caught by customs agents, or "held up" as they say. We heard the tale many times and by now it is a part of Caribbean folklore. The details change—the name of the ship, the size of the cargo, as well as the island where it reportedly took place—but it always begins when a captain returns from Saint Barts with a full hold, drops his anchor and rows ashore to find a customs agent waiting for him on the beach.

"Now row me to the boat," the official ordered.

The captain obliged, but halfway there an oar jumped out of a rowlock, went overboard, and floated away.

As the customs agent groped for the oar, the captain leaned to the same side, and suddenly the dinghy overturned. The two men swam to shore and pulled the swamped boat up on the beach.

"I'm terribly sorry," apologized the captain.

The customs agent looked at him sceptically, then at his schooner still riding at anchor in the bay. "It doesn't change anything," he replied.

"We can get some dry clothes at my house," the captain offered as he led the way.

"But I can't appear without my uniform," said the customs agent.

"Don't worry, my wife will hang it in the sun. In the meantime let's have a drink."

They wrapped themselves in towels and the captain put a bottle of rum on the table. Like gentlemen, they drank to each other's health, and every time the captain poured some more rum in the agent's glass, the captain's wife poured some more water on his uniform.

The clothes were still wet when the bottle was dry.

The moment the customs agent began to snore, the captain quietly sneaked out of the house, went back to the beach and unloaded his cargo.

"Don't think they always get off scot free," said John. "Every once in a while a smuggler is held up. Just the same, for them it's worth the risk. That's the only way a schooner can really make money."

We watched the agent, briefcase in hand, climb on board the *Albert George.* Trying to stay clean, he scrambled carefully over oil drums, gas bottles, and sacks of cement. In the stern he found a bit of shade on the bulwarks, spread out his white handkerchief and sat on it. The captain joined him and the two men began to pore over a sheaf of papers.

"Too bad you can't listen to that conversation," said John. "It would teach you something about the trade. What would probably surprise you the most is the fact that those schooners still make a profit. Not for the captain or the crew, but for everyone else. You see, everybody cheats them. It's so easy. Put more than three figures on a piece of paper and one of those captains is confused. An agent can pay him what he likes, a half, a third. There are hardly any limits on how far he can go. The captains have to have the cargo and the agent is the only one who can give it to him. So the more an agent can steal, the more cargo he gives the Captain.

"Sometimes the captains think they're being cheated; in fact, they always do. They're always complaining about the money, but they're never quite sure how the agent does it.

"But the games won't last much longer. The trade is growing fast and more and more of it is coming to ironboats like mine. The schooners won't be around for long. It's going to be a sad day for the agents when the last schooner gives up the trade."

That night we sailed on the *Albert George* bound for Grenada, and as Tub predicted, it was a rough passage. Short, choppy seas sent curtains of spray across the deck and a new squall seemed to arrive every hour on the hour.

We spent the night on deck, wrapped in an old sail and using a pile of crates as a dodger. The captain stood at the wheel a few meters away, and since we were within easy shouting distance, even in the midst of a squall, he chattered to us constantly. Tub was right. The captain did repeat his stories; in fact, we heard some of them two and three times before he gave the wheel to Tub at dawn.

We stayed in Grenada for three days, discharging cargo and painting the boat. At first we tried to paint in the way in which we were accustomed, sanding and scraping the surface, cleaning it, and then carefully applying the paint. But Tub thought we were working too slowly and gave us a quick lesson. Soon we were one with the crew splashing great quantities of paint over rust, dirt, grease, or whatever else came into the path of our brushes.

With the boat half painted—gray, white, blue, and yellow—we sailed on to Carriacou, a dependency of Grenada thirty-five miles to the north. Many of the fastest schooners are built there, most of them by descendants of Scottish shipwrights who originally settled the island. Names like McLaren, MacLawrence, MacFarland, and

Compton can still be found in the villages and the orientation toward the sea is traditional.

Carriacou is also probably the most well-known smuggling *entrepôt* in the Windward Islands. "Carriacouans have been smuggling for hundreds of years," one retired captain explained. "You don't expect us to stop now, do you?"

And it is quite evident that they don't plan to stop. Cheap liquor and cigarettes are thought to be the island's largest export and the supply appears inexhaustible. Shops in Hillsborough are always well stocked and Grenadian market women, or "speculators," as they are called, regularly come over by schooner to buy their goods at half price. When the boat leaves on the return voyage, dustbins by the quay are usually stuffed with cartons stenciled "Saint Barts."

On the other side of the island, facing northward, is the wide bay of Windward, a mile of sandy beach that for centuries has served as a schooner shipyard. The village itself is small, a string of simple, frame houses and bars that follows the curve of the beach. Above it, overlooking the bay, is the stone house of Julius McGarry, perhaps the most well-known shipwright in the Windward Islands.

Modest and soft-spoken, he is unusually fit for a man in his early sixties. Only his battered hands reveal his age. He seldom sails on any of the schooners he builds and only rarely has he ever left the island. He prefers a quiet life ashore, surrounded by his most prized possessions, the models of the ships he has built.

"No one taught me how to build boats," he told us. "No one really needed to. It's in the blood and has been for generations.

That's the Scottish part, I think. They came over hundreds of years ago, a whole group of shipwrights from Glasgow and settled here in Windward."

We joined him on the porch and moved two chairs into the shade.

Julius swept his arm across the panorama. "The beach and the water may be the same," he said, "but Carriacou was a very different place in those days. This island was one of the main ports in the sugar trade and windjammers were coming and going all the time. It wasn't unusual to have eight or ten of them anchored down there in the bay. Strange, isn't it? We were more in touch with the world then than we are today. Ships came straight from Europe loaded with furniture, wine, everything you can think of. What's here now? You can see for yourselves—just a couple of schooners and a few fishing dinghies. We're lucky if we can get a few boxes of nails from Trinidad.

"You see, all that high living didn't last long. The sugar industry gave out, then nobody came at all. We were left on our own. That's when we started to build ships, schooners, I mean, to trade with the other islands. We had to. It was either that or starve. And we've been building them ever since.

"Those first boats were different from the ones we have today. Most of them carried more sail, and they were pretty rough too. Nobody bothered to do much sanding or polishing or scrape away the tar. Beauty didn't count for much then. Little by little, we've made changes, narrowed the hull, added a transom, shaped the corners, things like that. A lot of shipwrights have thought about how those schooners should look.

Construction is always slow. By the time the hull is finished it has already taken on a weathered, seawise look.

"People often say 'in Carriacou they build better boats than houses.' That's probably true. The last hurricane that came through broke up a lot of the village. Roofs went everywhere. But we didn't lose a single boat.

"My father built schooners all his life and never drew a single plan. He'd sit on the beach for a day or so and work it all out in his head. Me, I have to do some calculations first, which is why I always make a model before I start."

He called to his wife and she brought him a model of the *Francis K*. It was about a meter long, perfect in every detail, and looked as if it had just been taken from a museum case. As he held the miniature schooner in his gnarled hands we wondered how he carved and fashioned the tiny blocks, pin rails, and fittings, all of which seemed so realistic and functional.

"I began building models when I was a kid," he explained. "I'd have a good look at the boat my father was building, then try to copy it. At that time all the kids in the village made models. It was a big competition. On weekends we'd have races along the beach. I usually had the fastest boat and neighbors would often ask me, 'Why don't you build bigger ones?'

"There wasn't anything else I wanted to do, and I've been constructing boats all my life."

"How many have you made?" we asked.

"Over the years I've built nineteen schooners, big ones, that is, fifty or sixty feet long overall. The last one was launched a few months ago, and I guess I'll be setting up the next one soon."

"What must you do before that?"

"The first thing to decide is how long she is going to be. Once you have the over-

all length, the rest can be calculated. It's all fairly simple."

Using his model of the *Francis K* as an example, he explained the simple formulas that determine a schooner's proportions.

"The beam should be about one-quarter the length," he said, "which means if your ship is to be sixty feet long, then her beam will be roughly fifteen feet. Now, if you halve the beam, you will have her draft, in this case about seven and a half feet. To find the height of the mast is also easy. Three times the beam (three by fifteen) plus the draft (seven and a half) equals the height of the main mast, fifty-two and a half feet. The foremast is usually a little shorter. I don't know why. It doesn't really have to be, except that that's the way we always do it and it does look nicer like that.

"The bowsprit is about the same length as the beam, but, of course, only two-thirds of it sticks out from the bow. That's all rather straightforward. In a couple of minutes you've got the basic dimensions. You may have to trim a little here and there so that she looks right, but generally I do that after I build the model.

"Now the problems begin. Perhaps the biggest one is to find the right wood. I don't mean the right kind. I mean the right shape. Each of the frames, from bow to stern, has to be cut from a cedar or mahogany tree that has roughly the shape we need. That's not so easy to find. I can spend days walking through the woods looking for stems and sterns and frames. Eventually, of course, we get all the wood and I choose a place on the beach where the boat can be easily launched and stack it there. The keel has to be sent for and that can take time too. Usually we use

it goes on like that for years. But if I can keep at it, and find four or five good workers to help me, I can build a schooner in about six months."

"You mean the hull, or the complete boat?"

"The boat, ready to sail. When she is almost ready, the owner chooses the launching date and that's what the whole island has been waiting for since the moment we laid the keel. Launching days are something special here, a little like carnivals, I guess. When we have one, everyone comes, from all the villages. You'd never think there were so many people on this little island. If it's a big boat, a full-sized schooner, then people will come from the other islands like Petite Martinique, Saint Vincent, and even Grenada."

"Just to have a good time?"

"They can't just play and drink. They have to work too. When the time comes to tow her into the water, everyone will be hauling on the ropes, pushing and shoving and straining. Of course, when they finish a feast will be waiting for them on the beach, so you could never say they aren't rewarded for their labors. Actually, the people who work the hardest on launch day are the cooks. They arrive at sunrise and slaughter all the animals—pigs, goats, and usually a bull too—and start cooking them in washtubs. Naturally, there is plenty of rum. There is never a shortage of that, especially here on Carriacou."

"And the launch?"

"Just before the launch, everyone becomes quiet and gathers around while the priest gives the boat a blessing, bringing the schooner into the world, so to speak. Like any baptism, there must be godparents and although I can't explain why, here

greenheart, which comes from Guyana."

"What kind of people ask you to build boats for them?"

"Most of them are in one type of business or another." He smiled. "Usually, it's the other. I'm sure you know what I mean. They have wild ideas about how they're going to make a fortune, and I suppose some of them do. But the one thing they all want is a bigger boat than they can afford. Owners often start boats before they have 'all the weight in their pocket,' that is, before they have all the money. That's okay with me, but when the money runs out, the work stops. Start, stop, sometimes

The West Indian schooner, a remnant of a great sailing fleet.

The Brazilian jangada—*only the basics: a raft, a sail, and a steering oar.*

The Chilean lancha chilota, *lumber sloops that sail in the gales of the roaring forties.*

The Egyptian aiyassa *still uses the river as a highway: upstream with the wind, downstream with the current. The cargoes: brick, limestone, and clay pots.*

The dam at Aswan has tamed
the Nile, now the weed creeps in.

The Sri Lankan oruwa—*a swift, sea-worthy outrigger canoe.*

The spritsail is tanned for protection against rot; the white panels, new untreated cloth.

The Bengali shampan, *a bulk carrier under sail.*

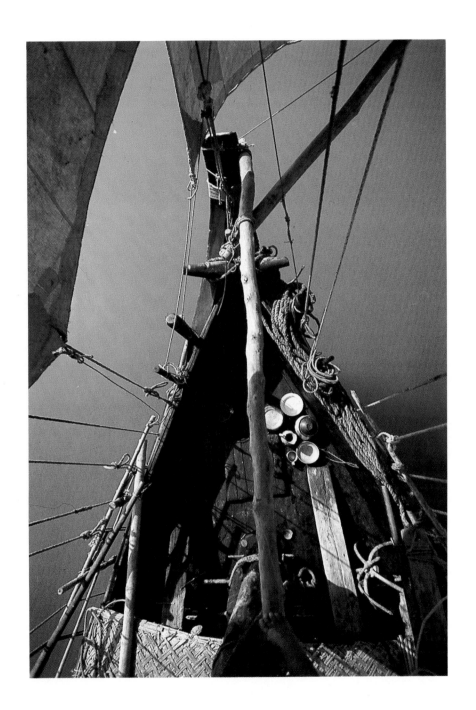

*The junk—the Chinese windjammer,
almost unchanged for thousands of years.*

The Indonesian pinisi—ships built by a different concept:
first the shell, then the skeleton.

on Carriacou they are always children.
They climb on the deck and stand beside
the priest while he sprinkles on the holy
water. As soon as he finishes, people cheer,
the drum rolls, and we sacrifice a goat at
the bow. We believe his spirit will lead the
schooner into the sea and always keep her
on course. To help push the boat into the
water and always keep her moving, we kill
a sheep at the stern and put a few drops of
its blood on the deck. When she floats and
I see her there in the bay riding at anchor,
I always get the feeling she's going to have
a prosperous life."

"Do you ever sail on any of your schooners?" we asked.

"No, almost never. In fact, I can't remember if I ever did. When they go into
the water and the sea trials are over they
pass out of my hands."

"But you do keep track of them?"

"No, not really."

We were astonished at his lack of interest in the fate of his schooners. It was almost as if, for him, their lives began and
ended on the shore. "You must get some
news of them occasionally?" we asked.

"From time to time one of them puts in
here for repairs, or a sailor gives me some
news. So far as I know every one of the
schooners I've built is still afloat today."

Two weeks later we sailed on the *Island
Queen* for Port of Spain. We helped the
crew set the sails and both of us noticed
that the schooner seemed to glide across
the choppy seas like a well-designed yacht.
We weren't surprised when the captain
told us she had been built in Carriacou by
Julius McGarry.

But the shipwright would not have been
glad to see his child. She had become a
tramp who wandered through the Windward Islands hauling whatever cargo she
could find. In need of paint, her fittings
and rigging rusted, her sails stained and
patched, she looked much older than her
age. Like many schooners, the *Island
Queen* had lost her regular trade to the
ironboats and, undoubtedly, would die
long before her time.

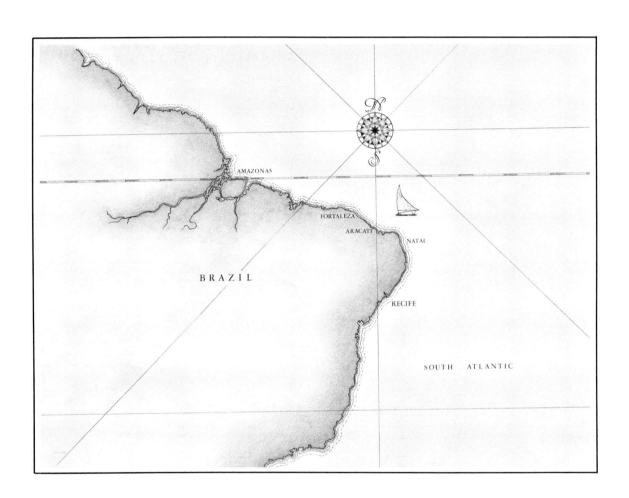

THE BRAZILIAN JANGADA

At first glance the Brazilian *jangada* resembles the kind of craft a castaway might hastily build to escape from a wreck or cannibals—just the bare essentials one needs to go to sea: a raft, a sail, and a steering oar. Logs awash, its blunt bow barely rising after each wave, the *jangada* seems to be on the verge of sinking. Easily one pictures Robinson Crusoe or the survivors of the *Medusa* clinging to its mast.

Undoubtedly it was on a similar craft that man first went to sea, and at one time sailing rafts could be found in many parts of the world—Peru, India, China, and the Pacific. Nearly all have vanished, most of them centuries ago. But in northeastern Brazil, the *jangada* still sails. It is one of the last, if not the last, of the breed.

Aside from a knife and a few fish hooks, not a single piece of iron or steel can be found on board. Despite four centuries of European contact, not a nail or a bolt is used in its construction. Plastic is also conspicuously absent, and, except for the muslin sail, so is any other manufactured product. The dipper used to wet the sail is hand carved, the basket that holds the catch, hand woven, and the cord that supports the mast and trims the sail, hand twisted.

The *jangadiero*, or fisherman, who stands on the stern holding the steering oar is also an anachronism. More than likely he cannot read. He wears no watch; his clothes are homemade. His home is a palm-thatched hut, and probably the furthest he has ventured from it is to the fishing grounds, some twenty or thirty miles offshore.

"How do the *jangadas* manage to survive?" We asked that question of many people.

"They were just overlooked," replied one Brazilian official. "For years the Northeast was like Amazonas, Brazil's forgotten backyard, and no one in Rio really cared what happened to a few colonies of fishermen. All that is changing now, of course."

"It's modern communication that's doing it," a sociologist in Recife explained. "You see, in many ways, *jangadieros* live in a closed society. Like the Indians, they're outcasts; they always have been. All they ask from us is to be left alone. And that's exactly what we can't do."

Only at sea does the *jangadiero* preserve his unique world. There, nearly out of sight of land, life is unchanged, tranquil, methodical, and, above all, silent. From the moment his *jangada* enters the surf until it emerges from it some twelve to sixteen hours later, hardly a word is ever spoken. The two or three men on board sail and fish together in a timeless rhythm that requires only an occasional gesture. Some say the sound of a human voice frightens away the fish, but more typically when

19

asked "Why the silence?" a *jangadiero* shrugs his shoulders as if to say, "Why? There is no 'why.' It has just always been so."

When the Portuguese arrived in Brazil in the fifteenth century they found the Indians on the northeastern coast poling a long, flat raft that they used to gather shellfish from reefs and lagoons. Fresh from discoveries in Asia, Portuguese sailors were reminded of a similar craft they had encountered in India called a *janga* and the word quickly became transmuted to *jangada*. Later, when the European population grew, and fish were in demand, the rafts were fitted with a sail and centerboard. But there the development stopped.

Nothing further was changed or added. The *jangadas* that sail today are virtually identical to those that were built nearly 400 years ago.

"There are still some of the old villages left," a harbormaster told us, "not many, but a few where the *jangadieros* live in the old way."

Those were the villages we sought, and traveling by car, launch, and foot, we followed the coast, stopping in every settlement we found. Most people didn't know where the villages were and those that did, didn't care. What we sought was obviously irrelevant information, like knowing the location of a gypsy camp. Since we were looking for something useless they could send us anywhere, and did. After a while we felt like census takers, for we always asked the same question: "Where are the *jangadas?*"

Early one afternoon we entered a small village at the end of one muddy, seldom-used road in Pernambucco and found a short, stocky man standing on the beach facing the sea. He was Jody de Silva, a community development officer, who is virtually the only contact the *jangadieros* have with the government. "Helping the unhelpable" is the way he refers to his profession. Before his present post he worked with Indians in the Amazonas, and before that with migrants in the slums of Rio.

Once a week he drives his battered Volkswagen down to the *jangadiero* village to see if there is anything in his limited power he can do for them. More than likely it will be nothing. But despite his pessimism, he has come to respect, and perhaps envy, the *jangadiero*'s way of life, and he is the first to lament the fact that very soon it will disappear.

Together we waited for the *jangadas* to arrive. They seemed to come in threes—three white triangles which would pop over the horizon and then waft toward us like handkerchiefs on the wind. Only when they neared the shore could we see that there were men on board.

They sailed parallel to the beach, waiting for just the right wave. One by one, they suddenly turned and shot the surf. As we watched them disappear into a curtain of foam and spray, then emerge safely on

the beach, Jody talked to us about the *jangadiero*'s plight.

"Every time I watch the *jangadieros* push their rafts into the surf they remind me of so many Don Quixotes setting out to conquer windmills. The big difference, I guess, is that the *jangadieros* don't really know who or what their windmills are, or perhaps, even that they are fighting at all. And it doesn't really matter anymore. That's the sad part. It's all a useless struggle. They were beaten a long time ago, and unfortunately, there is little that can be done about it. The world the *jangadieros* know is falling apart piece by piece, and only now when it's too late are some of them beginning to discover it.

"It's not just a matter of one technology replacing another—the change from sail to motor—a whole culture is being wiped out. Here, right on this beach. And there's not much we can do to stop it."

"Is it hopeless?" we asked.

"The root of the problem is economics. Small-scale fishing doesn't pay. It's as simple as that. The *jangadiero* works perhaps fifteen, sixteen hours a day, using six or seven of them to sail out to the fishing grounds. Can you imagine a worker in town spending half a day going to and from the factory? Never. He'd rather be unemployed. A *jangadiero* never thinks about it. He even sculls out when there is no wind, which, of course, takes even longer. I suppose that's why I feel sorry for them. All that work and they get so little for it.

"On a good day a *jangadiero* will come back with five or ten kilos of fish to sell, maybe half of it of the first quality. Waiting for him on the beach are the middlemen, each with his own percentage. What

profits there are will go to them. You can be sure of that. At best, the *jangadiero* will go home with 1,000 *cruzieros* [about $1.00] in his pocket. That's not much, is it? Don't bother to calculate the hourly wage. It's ridiculous. And quite often it's nothing, or maybe just a couple of fish to feed his family.

"In any case, he can never get ahead. If he doesn't have his own boat and works for another *jangadiero* as crew, it's virtually hopeless. He's no different than a share-cropper who will never own anything more valuable than a new machete.

"If he owns his *jangada*, he's a little better off, but not much. He's still got a hell of a struggle just to stay afloat. Don't forget, a *jangada* only lasts about a year, then you have to get fresh logs and build a new one."

This simple fact—that the raft must be replaced every year—is perhaps the greatest threat to the *jangadiero*'s existence. The *peuba* (Apeiba Tibuou) logs that make up the raft are porous and absorb sea water. Sometimes the exposed ends are given a coat of paint, but this adds no more than a few months to the raft's lifespan at best. Gradually, the *jangada* becomes water-logged, and when it is more awash than afloat, the *jangadiero* has no choice but to abandon it. He salvages the mast, sail, benches, and centerboard, then builds himself a new raft.

Thus a *jangada* is not a "boat" in the Western sense of the word, that is, a craft that is blessed, given a name and often an anthropomorphic personality. To the *janga-diero* his sailing raft is a disposable tool, a vehicle that has but a short life and is then discarded. A new *jangada* is usually slipped into the water without so much as a toast

in its honor, and rarely is it ever dignified with a name.

At one time, obtaining fresh *peuba* logs posed no problem. Resembling balsa, the tree is easy to cut and trim, and a man can carry two or three logs on his shoulder for quite a distance without difficulty. *Peuba* grew in the shade of the dense jungle and was found everywhere.

But in the late nineteenth century the railroads arrived, and when the price of coal rose, wood became the fuel. Whole forests were destroyed. That, and the steady encroachment of farm land, nearly eliminated the jungle. *Peuba* now grows in only a few locations, and naturally the price has skyrocketed. For the logs that make up the raft the *jangadiero* must pay about $100—not much perhaps for a Western wallet, but for a fisherman who is not fully part of the money economy, it is exorbitant and nearly prohibitive.

The scarcity of *peuba* has already produced a hybrid, a new species of *jangada* that is found mainly in the state of Ceara. The *jangadieros* there imported their *peuba* from Pernambucco to the south, and when the price rose dramatically in the 1950s, they began building *jangadas* with whatever wood they could find. The result was the *jangada de tabua*, a *jangada* of planks, which has roughly the same shape as the log raft, but is a true hull, planked and caulked. It also has two other refine-ments—at sea the steering oar is replaced by a rudder, and a small jib has been added for maneuverability. Naturally, a *jangada de tabua* is more expensive, about three or four times that of a *peuba jan-gada*, but it will last longer if well main-tained.

When asked which he prefers, a *janga-*

Each log is tapered and cut into a V to give the raft a semblance of form.

Twice a day the jangada *must be rolled across the beach to and from its berth above the high water mark.*

diero typically replies, "*Peuba.*" Whether this is nostalgia or the fact that a log raft, especially when waterlogged, is a more stable fishing platform, is difficult to ascertain. Perhaps the *jangadiero* just feels more secure on his traditional *peuba* raft. "No matter what happens at sea," he says, "it can't sink."

As we walked along the beach with Jody we saw a dozen or more *jangadas* scattered across the sand and nearly every breaker brought more of them surfing onto the beach. The *jangadieros* waved to Jody,

then pushed their rafts toward thatch-roofed sheds just beyond the high-water mark. They used palm logs as rollers and the system could not be more simple. Only two logs are used, and as soon as the raft rolls over one of them, like a game of leap frog, someone runs ahead and puts the other one in the path.

"Add a bit of inflation to the price of *peuba*," Jody continued, "and you have a situation where every year the *jangadiero's* new raft costs him thirty or forty percent more than it did the year before. That kind of spiral cannot go on for very long. Nowadays as soon as a *jangadiero* gets some money he buys a log or two and stores them away for his next raft. But that doesn't really help. His catch isn't any larger than it was—if anything, it's smaller—and as for the price of fish, well, as I mentioned before, there is a long distance between wholesale and retail prices.

"Of course, the *jangadiero* doesn't know much about prices. He's not a businessman. A sharp fish buyer can run circles around him, and they do every day.

"But his real enemy, the one that will finally put him out of business, is the diesel-engine launch that is sailing right alongside him and fishing in the same waters. With the same crew as a *jangada*—two or three men—a motor launch will haul in at least six or seven times more fish, and in half the time. You can't survive with competition like that.

"So, you see, there's not a lot one can do for the *jangadieros*. I've been working with them here in Pernambucco for five years. Sometimes I can get them a small loan or some medical help, or maybe some advice on where to fish, but that's not really much, and it certainly doesn't take care of their windmills."

"Is there no other solution?" we asked.

"None that I know of," Jody replied. "At one time we looked around for possibilities, a new way to fish, or something like that, but obviously we haven't been very successful. It seems like there should be an answer. After all, the *jangada* has been around for a long time, probably because it's a very adaptable craft. But how do you make a *jangada* more efficient? Put an outboard motor on it? People have tried that, but it doesn't work for very long.

Usually the vibrations tear the raft apart. Anyway, if you have the money to buy an outboard motor, you can probably afford a proper boat as well.

"Another thing that often happens, especially to those villages that are near a city, is that some rich businessman or politician comes along, sees what a lovely beach the *jangadieros* have, and decides to put up a house where he can spend the weekends. He offers a *jangadiero* more money than he's seen in his life for his little plot on the beach and naturally he accepts it. So the guy builds a vacation house, and when it's finished his friends come down for the weekend, and they see what a lovely beach it is. Before long, there's a hardtop road, shops, and restaurants, and a beach full of fancy homes, which, of course, are usually boarded up. The *jangadieros* and their families have moved behind the dunes, next to the swamp, or anywhere else where the land has no value. They may try to hang on for a while, but there's really no point. Usually they end up working on construction, building more houses, or else they go to the city to live in a *favela* [slum].

"Faced with all this, you ask, 'Can the *jangadiero* survive?' I doubt it; in fact, I know he can't. It's impossible. Everybody is running as fast as they can to develop the Northeast. The poor *jangadiero* is going to get everything at once—roads, buses, electricity, TV, you name it. He's going to become a part of the system whether he likes it or not."

"How much longer does he have?"

"I couldn't say exactly. Three years, five, a bit more, perhaps. But certainly within ten years the only *jangada* you'll find in Brazil will be in a museum. *E'o que sei.* [That is what I know.]"

After the last *jangada* crossed the beach, we followed Jody to one of the sheds. Three *jangadas* were inside, two lying on their sides and one resting on its rollers. Ashore, they looked more fragile and elemental than ever. While Jody chatted with the *jangadieros*, taking care of his business, we sat on the *jangada* and looked at it carefully.

Its simplicity is deceptive. On closer inspection each of the basic parts—the raft, mast, and sail, and the steering oar—is much more sophisticated than it at first appears.

The *jangada*'s construction has little in common with the crude raft Robinson Crusoe hastily built. Five, six, or eight logs are used, depending on the overall length; the longer the raft, the more logs are needed for stability. Each log is shaped, tapered fore and aft, and cut in the form of a V with the point downward. At four or five points along its length, holes are drilled through the logs and a limb of hardwood, *Ibiribi* (Ibira Vermelha), is wedged through them like a dowel. The result is a rigid structure, a semblance of a

The simplicity of the sail resembles that of a modern racing dinghy.

The raft is held together by dowels, and a dozen or more hardwood "arrows" wedge them in place.

boat, more like a skow than a clipper ship, but a hull nonetheless. With a good wind a *jangada* sails easily at five to six knots, which is roughly the cruising speed of a sailboat of comparable length.

The mast has an unusual refinement that one would expect to find on a modern racing yacht, but certainly not on a "primitive" sailing craft. It can be stepped in any of eleven positions—in a center hole perpendicular to the deck, and in five other holes on each side. Two of the five incline the mast toward the wind. Thus, with a beam wind the raft sails with a minimum

Each hole is a mast step, enabling the jangadiero to alter the position of the sail with respect to the wind.

of heel and a maximum of sail area. The stronger the wind, the more the mast is leaned toward it. The other three holes form a triangle slightly aft and are used when sailing close to the wind. In addition to keeping the mast erect, the center of the sail area is moved forward, thereby compensating to some extent for the lack of a foresail.

By simply dropping the mast in the right hole, the *jangadiero* achieves roughly the same effect a modern yachtsman does when he changes and trims his sails. Where and how this ingenious method originated no one knows, but it is certainly unique. No other native craft in the Americas has ever used such a system.

The *jangada*'s steering arrangement is another novel device. A large hardwood knob is attached to the stern and the steering oar is placed against it, held there by the craft's leeway. Thus the oar always corrects for the natural tendency of the raft to fall off the wind. To adjust the amount of

helm, a *jangadiero* raises or lowers the blade.

Through Jody we met many *jangadieros*, among them Roberto, who invited us to stay with him. His house was identical to others in the small village: mud and wattle walls, thatch roof, and a sand floor. A half-dozen partitions divided the house into rooms and we slung our hammocks in the kitchen, sharing it with two small children and a large army of mosquitos. The children slept soundly while we unsuccessfully battled a more voracious life form.

As far back as Roberto knows, at least four generations, the men in his family have been *jangadieros*. But this seems to be at an end. Although he has seven children, all of them are girls, and Roberto often said he is "a guest in a house of women."

We stayed with Roberto for two weeks and took turns sailing with him. Early in the morning we helped him roll the *jangada* down the beach and push it into the surf. At the last minute, as the sail caught the wind and the raft passed through the breaking waves, one of us jumped on board.

We fished as best we could, and often our awkward attempts to control the lines were more a source of amusement than a rewarding activity.

Since *jangadieros* rarely speak at sea, it was only in the evenings after a dinner of fish and rice that we had a chance to talk. Roberto would sit in a hammock, usually with a child or two asleep in his lap, and tell us stories of the sea.

"Sometimes there are storms, that's true, and the dangerous part is the wind. It's not the sea that has the power, no, the sea is the slave of the wind. It's the wind who says, 'calm down' or 'rise up,' and it's the wind that brings the rain and then sends it away to let the sun shine. That's why I always watch the wind before I sail. Or at least I do now. When I was younger, I wasn't so wise. Like everybody else, I made my mistakes. Not long after I got my first *jangada*, years and years ago, I sailed out to the *paredes* [the edge of the continental shelf] during the rainy season. There were three of us on board: Joao, Gispin, and I, all young and ready to take our chances. We hoped to come back with lots of big fish when everybody else had just little ones."

Two of the older girls came into the room, and quietly sat on the floor. We discovered later that they seldom heard their father talk about his adventures at sea. As women, they had no part in that side of his life. Roberto's stories were as new to them as they were to us.

"The other *jangadas* only went as far as the reef," Roberto continued, "and I re-member passing my uncle who was anchored there. He waved and gestured toward the sky. I knew what he was saying, but it was only later that I found out what he meant.

"We had just finished fishing when the storm hit. Our basket was full, and we had six or seven tunas, big ones, tied to the bench. Suddenly, the sea became strange, and in all the years that I've been sailing I've never seen it like that again. The waves were steep, almost like cliffs, and seemed to come from everywhere. Sometimes two waves met, and sent water flying in all directions. I remember it went on for an hour or so like that, getting worse and worse. Everywhere I looked the sea was white. Then, all of a sudden, the *jangada* fell, as if we had gone over the edge and there was nothing beneath us. We went down head first. The bow rammed into the water and over we went.

"When I came up the *jangada* was floating upside down about twenty meters away. I swam over and climbed on top of it. Joao was already there, but we never saw Gispin again. He was a good swimmer, so I guess something must have hit him when the *jangada* turned over. Joao and I clung to the logs and the waves rolled over us."

Roberto paused for a moment to make room in the hammock for another one of his girls. She leaned against him and quickly fell asleep.

A capsize on the open ocean is perhaps the greatest danger a *jangada* faces. Obviously, a raft floats equally well whichever side is up. Mast down and drifting in a heavy sea, a *jangada* can be an unwieldy craft. After freeing the mast and sail, a *peuba jangada* can usually be righted by the weight of its three-man crew and a fillip from a passing wave. But that which sounds simple in theory can often be impossible in practice, especially in an angry sea, and an old *jangada*, water heavy and nearly at the end of its life, will right much easier than a new buoyant one.

"Whenever we got the chance," Roberto continued, "we tried to turn the raft right side up, but she was too heavy for just the two of us. I still had my knife, so I climbed on board, lay down, and cut through the *clavos* [hardwood dowels that bind the logs together] to free one of the *mimburas* [outer logs]. After it drifted away, we managed to turn the raft over without much trouble."

Of course, this technique will not work with a *jangada de tabua*, which has a planked hull. When one of these turns turtle, a crew member swims to the stern where there is a small plug for just such an emergency. He opens it, allows the boat to half-fill, then replaces the plug. Using the weight of the water, and a wave as a fulcrum, the *jangada de tabua* can be quickly righted.

"But that wasn't the end of it all," Roberto went on. "Everything was gone, mast, sail, fish, and our lines too. We tied ourselves to the bench and just waited for the storm to end. That night was the worst and the longest I've ever spent at sea. Later, the waves calmed down a little, but the wind never did. It screamed the whole night. But the worst of it was the cold. We hardly said a word, Joao and I; we just sat there and shivered. Whenever we couldn't stand it any longer, we went back into the water and hung onto the raft. That was the only way to warm up.

"We saw the coastline in the morning,

The killick, a primitive wood and stone anchor, was once common on sailing craft all over the world.

and the current slowly took us toward it. Just before sunset we washed up on the beach. We didn't know where we were, but there was a *jangadiero* village not far away. They were good people and we stayed with them for a few days. We made a new mast and boom, that wasn't hard, and we found an old *peuba* log to replace the one we cut off. A *jangadiero* loaned us a sail to take us home. Fortunately, accidents like that don't happen often. Once is enough for a lifetime."

"But you still sail out to the *paredes?*"

"Sometimes. That's where the best fish are, but usually I only go about twenty kilometers, to where we went today."

"Do you always fish with lines?"

"I'd rather fish with a net, but they're expensive these days. If you're fishing with a line you've got to wait until a hungry fish comes along, but if you've got a net, you get them whether they're hungry or not. But we don't have a net. So we just sit there like we did today and wait for the fish to get hungry."

Fishing with the mast down, a *jangada* often has a stark, forlorn appearance.

When seen from a distance, silhouetted against the sky, the men on board can easily look more like ragged castaways than working fishermen. Confusion is almost inevitable, and has occurred quite often.

"Sometimes you see big boats far away on the horizon," Roberto told us, "and you watch them cross from one side to the other. It helps to pass the time. Once a funny thing happened. One of the big boats changed course and sailed right toward us. When it was close, it stopped and lowered a boat. Six or seven men rowed over. They waved and shouted a lot, but I couldn't figure out what they wanted. We waved. They waved. Finally the man in the bow pointed to his mouth as though he were hungry. I took a big *cavalo* we had

just caught and threw it to him. He laughed, then threw me some cigarettes. So I threw him another fish. Then everybody threw us cigarettes. In a few minutes they had all our fish and we had all their cigarettes. That was the best catch we've ever had.

"Now every time we go out I watch the big boats and hope we'll meet some more hungry sailors."

Roberto carried his children, one by one, to their hammocks. Then he waved a goodnight to us and blew out the kerosene lamp.

The next morning he woke us at three and handed us cups of cold coffee. Leftover rice served as breakfast. Then we walked down to the beach and rolled the *jangada* across the sand. It was only when the surf slapped us in the face that we really woke up. Soon we were completely wet, sailing and shivering in the dark, and constantly looking seaward for the sun's first warming rays.

At the fishing grounds, perhaps fifteen miles from shore, not a sail was in sight. We bobbed in the uneven Atlantic swell and the waves washed over the raft leaving behind cords of foam. Suddenly we had a stark realization: we were cut off from civilization and hurled back not centuries but millennia. We were tempting the sea with only a crude, almost primeval, log raft.

About midday the wind backed and we hoisted sail. As we neared the coast we joined other *jangadas* and as a group the tiny fleet of rafts headed toward the surf and the beach.

We spent four hours that day at the fishing grounds, and caught perhaps thirty fish. One man marked his fish by cutting off half the tail, another by cutting the fin. Only Roberto's fish went into the basket whole since he is the captain. The catch is rarely large, we learned, about ten to fifteen kilos on the average, just enough to feed the *jangadieros* and their families, with perhaps a little left over for their wives to sell in the market.

The *jangadas* usually return to shore just after midday. More than half their time at sea has been spent sailing to and from the fishing grounds. Occasionally the wind dies and a *jangada* is left stranded, drifting with the current to spend the night at sea. Like any other craft, the captain or *mestre* has his privileges. He raises the steering oar, lashes it across the bench, and sleeps on it. The two crew sleep below, so to speak, sit-

ting up and tied to the bench legs or the mast.

Jangadas have been known to travel long distances in this manner, sailing during the day, drifting at night. The longest documented voyage took place in 1951 when five *jangadieros* sailed from Ceara and arrived safely in the south of Brazil, some 2,000 miles and two months later. The reason for the voyage is unclear. Sheer adventure, perhaps; but more likely it was a

desperate attempt to call attention to conditions in the impoverished Northeast.

In any case, little help was forthcoming. The *jangadiero* villages remain, as they always have been, poor, marginal, and isolated. The only change is that every year there are fewer and fewer of them.

Taking away both the fish and the markets are diesel-engined launches that harvest quantities of fish the *jangadieros* never dreamed were there.

The *jangadiero* cannot compete, and by comparison his efforts seem futile and absurd.

Today, just to feed his family and purchase logs for his *jangada*, he must work harder than ever before, and in this there is

a sad irony. Popular belief has it that the *jangadiero* leads an indolent life of ease. The sea is full of fish, so the saw goes, and a *jangadiero* has only to curtail his siesta and sail out to scoop them up.

Nothing could be further from the truth.

Whichever direction the *jangadiero* looks, to the sea or to the shore, he faces problems he cannot possibly hope to surmount. Clearly he faces extinction, and quite likely he has begun to sense it. The signs are just too many and too overwhelming. The shadow of his *jangada* lengthens on the beach and one day soon it will not be there.

On our way back to Recife we stopped to swim at Boa Viagem, a former *jangadiero* village that has become an exclusive suburb. Glass and concrete apartment houses line the beach front and a four-lane highway leads straight into the center of the city. The only thing that remains of the original village is its name.

We were surprised to find a half-dozen *peuba jangadas* sharing the beach with the sunbathers. The *jangadieros* formed an incongruous island of the past and sat in the shade of a palm tree drinking beer. There we met Ernesto, the doyen of the group. Although well over sixty, he is still strong and agile, very much an old man of the sea. Somehow he still manages to think of Boa Viagem as it was, and always he speaks of it as "my beach."

"We used to watch Recife grow," he told us, "first one building, then another, and another. Then they built the road and people used to come out here to swim. We lived over there, where that blue building is now." He pointed to a huge apartment house with pastel balconies and brown-tinted windows. "Nothing was here then, just a lot of sand and our village. It was a small one, about thirty houses, and we were all *jangadieros*. In those days there were more *jangadas* on this beach than palm trees. Those were good times for us. We sold fish, and some people would drive all the way out from the city just to buy from us.

"One day an official came and told us we had to leave. He gave everyone a piece of paper that said they owned the land and there was nothing we could do about it. No one believed him until the bulldozers arrived. Then it was too late. In an hour or so nothing was left.

"We moved to the *favela* on the other side of Recife and I come here every day by bicycle. I've been doing it for five years now. It's a long way, I know, but I wouldn't go anywhere else. I still think of this place as my beach. It isn't mine, of course, I know that. It never was, but that's the way I feel about it.

"I do what everyone else does here. I take people out for a sail. We don't go far, just along the reef, perhaps for an hour or so. Five hundred *cruzieros* [about three dollars] is what I try to get, but sometimes I have to take less. It all depends on how it goes. Saturdays and Sundays are usually my best days, but not every week finishes with a good weekend."

"Do you ever go fishing?" we asked.

"I'm still a fisherman. That's what I always have been. I go fishing whenever I

can. I'd go more often, but the sea is different now, and it seems I always come back with less and less fish. It's just not worth it. The fish aren't there anymore. Besides, I have to admit that when the tourists are here their money comes quicker. One tourist is as good as five kilos of the best fish, and it's a lot less work to catch them."

"Is that enough money to live on?"

"No, but I even make a little money just sitting here on the beach. It's not much, but it comes in regularly at the beginning of each month. I only have to hoist my sail in the morning and leave it up all day so that people can see what's written on it. The business started a couple of years ago, and now you won't find a single *jangada* on this beach without something written on its sail—beer, cigarettes, toothpaste, even banks put their names on them. We get the sails for nothing, all painted and ready to go.

"It's good to have the extra money. I need it. But sometimes when I sail close to the beach I feel a bit uneasy, like I wish I could turn away or hide behind the sail. I know people aren't looking at me, just at the sign on my sail, but I don't like it just the same.

"I have six sons and none of them will be a *jangadiero*. I don't blame them. Why should they go fishing when they can make five, ten times more money in town. And the same is true for the rest of the fishermen. Their houses are empty too, sons and daughters all gone off to the cities to become rich.

"There are no young *jangadieros* here. We're all old men on this beach. Carlos, over there, is the youngest, fifty-two, and one day he'll probably be the only one taking the tourists out for a sail. I wouldn't like to change places with him.

"To be alone at sea is one thing, to be left alone on the beach is another."

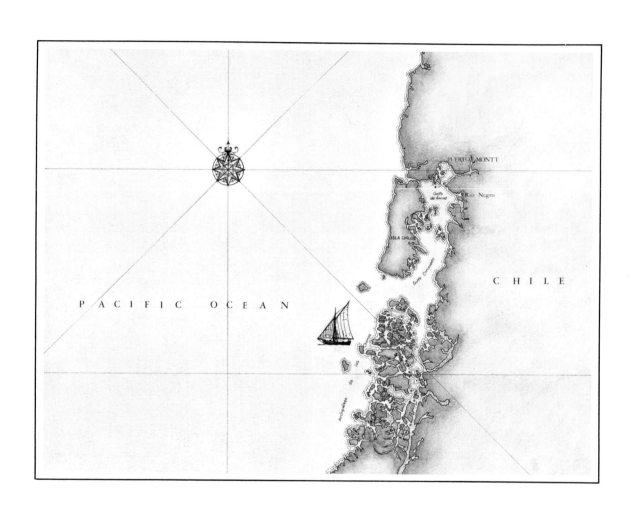

THE CHILEAN
LANCHA CHILOTA

In the stormy, cold waters of Chiloe the lumber trade, one of the oldest windjammer businesses, still thrives. From remote coastal villages on the edge of the Andes, a small fleet of gaff-rigged sloops regularly ferries rough-cut planks, shingles, and firewood to the markets of Puerto Montt and Calbucco.

Located in the south of Chile where the land mass ends and the islands begin, the region of Chiloe includes the island of that name, the adjacent coastline, called Chiloe continental, and the archipelago between the two. It is not large, roughly the size of Cyprus, and marks the limit of the Chilean frontier. From Chiloe southward, all the way to Tierra del Fuego, the land is sparsely populated, undeveloped, and desolate.

The sailing conditions are among the world's worst: a rocky, jagged coast dotted with islands, high tides, few navigation lights, and a severe, inhospitable climate. "Cold, squalls, and fog" is the normal forecast. It rains over 300 days a year and from whichever direction the wind blows it is likely to be unpleasant: from the North and East it sweeps off the snow-covered Andes, from the South it carries the chill of Cape Horn and Antarctica, and from the West it brings Pacific storms out of the "Roaring Forties." The region has only two seasons, winter and summer, the former lasting perhaps ten months or more,

and the latter merely a break between the storms.

Chiloe has always been regarded as a place apart, and not just because of the bad weather. The Chilotes, as the people are called, were one of the few groups in the pre-Columbian Americas to have a nautical tradition, one that they still maintain today. For them, the sea has always been a highway and a vital source of food.

When the Spanish arrived in the sixteenth century they found Chilote sailors fishing and trading along the coast in large open rowboats called *dalkas*. The craft resembed a flat-bottomed canoe and was a model of simplicity. Three rough planks—one for the bottom and two for the sides—were sewn together with grass cord and caulked with bark. The boat held eight to ten people, and reportedly at least two of them bailed constantly. But what the *dalka* lacked in seaworthiness, it made up for in practicability. Whenever the boat was not needed, the planks were easily unlashed and stored ashore.

The Spanish introduced the sail and, since it proved impossible to rig a *dalka*, the Chilotes soon abandoned their leaky rowboats and began to copy the beamy *caravels*. Over the centuries they made a few modifications. The hull was flattened so that the boat could dry out in the tidal waters, the ornamental woodwork gradually disappeared, and a gaff rig replaced the

original square and lateen sails. But the *caravel* is there, in form, if not in fact, and the *lancha chilota*, which is still being built by hand, is perhaps its only living descendant.

In Puerto Montt, the last town before the wilderness, we boarded the *Cruz del Sur*, the weekly ferry that is the only regular link between Chiloe continental and the outside world.

As usual, the weather was stormy. Short, choppy seas covered the windows with spray and a new squall seemed to arrive every hour. After a rough passage across the Gulf of Ancud, the small ferry passed into the lee of the mountains and snaked along the coast, stopping at nearly every inlet and headland to let off passengers and cargo.

We remained on board until the last stop, Rio Negro, a tiny, forlorn settlement at the end of a long fjord. Two dozen clapboard shacks formed a semicircle around the water's end, and on all sides the forested land rose steeply to the snow-tipped Andes. Several *lanchas chilota* were beached on the rocky shore, loading lumber at low tide.

We asked one of the captains when he was going to sail.

"When the wind is right," he replied, and introduced himself as Osvaldo, the *patron* or owner of the *Anita*.

Like other captains in Chiloe, Osvaldo has one boat in the sea and the other ashore. Further down the coast he has a small plot of land where he and his family raise potatoes, graze sheep, and just manage to survive. Osvaldo sails because he must—it is the only way he knows to augment his meager income.

His *lancha chilota* is homemade, rough in appearance and lacking in symmetry. No plans were ever drawn, not even a sketch in the sand, and the eye often failed, for port and starboard halves do not match. The fittings are few and most have been salvaged from scrap. Steel reinforcing rods serve as chain plates, angle-iron has been hammered into rudder pintles, and the shrouds are a patchwork of line, chain, and rusted cable joined by a fantasy of knots. Even the running rigging was improvised or simply fashioned from whatever was on hand. Branches were bent into mast-hoops, and the rope for sheets and halyards hand twisted or cut from rawhide. The only items that Osvaldo purchased were the canvas for the sails and fifty kilos of nails.

While we were waiting for the tide to fall, we sat on *Anita*'s deck and talked with Osvaldo and his son about the lumber trade.

"Why are you so interested in the *lanchas?*" he asked.

"We'd like to sail up the coast on one."

"It's quicker to go by horse," he replied. "And easier too. If you get cold you can always stop somewhere to warm up."

"We'd prefer to go by boat."

He let the subject drop, but from time to time we noticed that he seemed to be scrutinizing us incredulously, as though trying to fathom why anyone would willingly travel by *lancha*, especially in the winter.

Later, as we were saying goodbye, he said, "You can sail with me if you like."

"When are you leaving?" we asked.

"As I told you before, when the wind is right."

Two days later the clouds parted and a herd of mare's tails announced a change in the weather. In a rare moment of sunlight we climbed on board *Anita*, cast off, and glided out into the bay. Then, suddenly, the wind died and the water became quiet and misty, more like a placid lake than an arm of the sea.

"There's wind farther down," Osvaldo said, pointing to the mouth of the fjord several miles away. "It's either wait or work," he said, picking up a long oar and making his choice known.

We launched the dinghy, paid out the tow rope, and all afternoon while Osvaldo and his son took turns sculling on the stern, we towed *Anita* toward the wind. It was slow, grueling work. The *lancha*, loaded with 10,000 shingles, rode deep in the water.

At dusk we were nearly exhausted and resting slumped over the oars when we felt the first whiff of a breeze. Osvaldo waved us back on board, and we quickly set the sails. Minutes later, *Anita* sailed out of the fjord and into the night.

The temperature dropped rapidly, perhaps ten degrees in as many minutes, and we huddled around a brazier of coals, drinking endless cups of *mate* and talking to forget the cold.

"In these waters if you wait for good weather you'll never sail," Osvaldo explained. "There isn't any, except in the summer and that doesn't last long. When the wind's from the south, like it is now, almost everyone sails with it."

He took a pair of socks from his pocket, slipped them over his hands, then took his turn at the tiller. Squatting low, he nearly disappeared into his *poncho* to protect himself from the wind.

"You usually know when the weather's going to change," he continued. "There

are lots of signs. One of the best is the *cordillera*. As long as the snow on the top stays white the weather won't change, but when it becomes gray, you know a storm is coming.

"You can even tell exactly when it is going to arrive. A few hours before it gets here the leaves of the *canelo* tree turn. The tops of them are green and the undersides white. I don't know why, but when rain is coming the leaves turn and the trees look white."

"But what happens if you're already at sea?" we asked.

"Nothing you can do about it then. Those things happen. Sooner or later everybody gets caught in dirty weather. You can usually wriggle out of it and get into the lee of an island, but your boat has to be in good shape—not too old and with no worms in her bottom. You never know about the worms. They can eat through new planks in a couple of months. But even with a strong boat you can still get into trouble. It happens all the time. They say twenty sailors drowned in Chiloe last year, and it wouldn't surprise me if it were true. We picked up someone just last month, not far from here. He had sailed over from Castro to buy a keel for a new boat. It was a big log he bought, about twenty meters, and he tied it behind his *lancha* and started to tow it across the Gulf. Then he got caught in a storm. With that log slowing him down, he didn't have time to get behind an island, and he didn't want to cut it loose either. He should have, though. That was his mistake. But when you pay 3,000 pesos [about $50] for a tree, you don't want to lose it.

"But he lost everything—the new keel and the old boat. He told us that a wave

During the short summer the whole family moves on board.

lifted up the log and hurled it through the stern of his *lancha*. She filled up with water and went down in a couple of minutes. The only thing that sailor didn't lose was his life. He was cold as hell when we found him, and I'm sure he couldn't have lasted much longer."

"Does anyone ever get accustomed to the cold here?" we asked.

"Not really. It's the wind that bothers me. No matter how many sweaters I have on, it seeps in and goes straight to my bones. That's the funny thing about sailboats. You're never warm with the wind and you can't sail without it. The best you can do is keep it behind you. That's best for you and the boat."

His son brought him a small brazier of coals and he put it between his boots, then threw his *poncho* over it. "That helps some," he said, "but, of course, it won't keep the wind off your back. Nothing will do that. And the worst of it is you sit here half warm, half cold, and sometimes I don't know which half feels worse."

The wind whipped beneath his *poncho* and sent a shower of sparks flying toward the mainsail. He laughed and gestured toward the sail. "That's why it has so many patches. Sometimes I wait too long before I throw the coals overboard. But when the weather's really bad, there's not much else to do except sit here and freeze and hope there will be a little sun in the morning to warm you up.

"It's not much better below. We don't

have berths, as you know. You just find a flat space somewhere and wrap up in a few sheepskins. Trouble is, they're always wet, and nothing dries slower than a sheepskin. When I'm shivering below I think I'll be warmer at the tiller, and when I'm on the tiller I wish I were below."

"How long does a voyage usually last?"

"No more than a couple of days. Since all the *lanchas* sail about the same time, we meet up in Puerto Montt. That's the only time I see my friends. Sure, we're all trying to sell the same thing, lumber, but it's not a real market. Almost everybody has their own buyers, and if there's some

wood left over, we don't fight about the price. If you have to stay an extra day or two to sell what's left, it doesn't matter. You can always find someone to drink and talk with.

"At home there's nobody to talk to except the family. The nearest neighbor is miles away and that's a long walk just for a little chat. It's better to sit by the stove and wait for someone to drop by.

"And they do sometimes. You never know who is going to knock at your door. If he's a sailor, then he's welcome, whether you know him or not. That's the custom here. Boats are always putting in somewhere to escape from a storm, and when they do, there's no need for the whole crew to suffer on board, so one or two go ashore. There's usually a farmhouse somewhere nearby. As long as the weather is bad, the sailors can stay and eat and sleep and share whatever you have. Tomorrow I may be knocking on their door."

"People in Puerto Montt told us . . ."

"Yes, I know what they think," he said, cutting us off. "They say that we work only when we're hungry, but that's a lie. They see us sitting on the *lanchas* selling wood and think that's all we do—just drink *mate* and talk to whoever comes along. But they haven't seen us at home. Where are you going to get the wood to sell if you don't cut it first? And getting wood on the *cordillera* is no easy job. Ask anyone. Ask them how many fingers they've chopped off. Ask them about the rheumatism they've got from working in the rain, and the sores on their feet. People get lost up there in the mountains, and they freeze to death sometimes too. Don't believe anybody who tells you we have an easy life. All that wood has to be chopped and sawed and dragged down by hand. It takes weeks to fill a *lancha*, and in the end you won't get all that much for it in Puerto Montt.

"I'm happy if after I buy the flour and paraffin and other things for the house I have enough left over to buy a few bottles of wine or have some drinks with my friends. Anyway, money's no good here. Everybody trades. That's the way we've always done it. These days the best thing to trade is *chicha* [new wine]. For a few bottles you can get a fat chicken anywhere. That's what I load up with—wine—as much as I can buy. I'd fill the boat if I could, and sail home loaded with *chicha*. But that's everybody's dream."

At dawn the *lancha*'s bow touched ground in front of Osvaldo's farmhouse, and, stiff and stumbling with cold, we beached the boat on the rocky shore. The smell of freshly baked bread wafted out of the chimney, and soon we were seated around the cast-iron stove, eating small, unleavened buns as fast as they came out of the oven.

Later Osvaldo showed us a trail that cut inland through the forest. Twenty kilometers further north, he told us, we would find several communities of woodcutters, and, of course, more *lanchas chilota*. He and his son would spend the next two weeks on the farm, cutting firewood to fill the rest of *Anita*'s beamy hold.

The trail was clearly marked but difficult to follow. Walking through Chiloe continental, we quickly discovered, was like plodding through a soggy, forested swamp. The ground was a sponge, and wherever we stepped we could feel water beneath us. After several hours the trail ended abruptly on the bank of a large river. Having little

choice, we followed it downstream and at its mouth found the remnants of a crude bridge that had obviously been washed away by a flood. There was a woodcutter's shack nearby and a small sailing dinghy was propped against it.

A small boy peered out of the door, then ran over to us.

"Where is your father?" we asked.

"In the *cordillera* cutting wood," he replied.

"When he comes back, do you think he would sail us to the other side?"

"I'll take you over at high tide," he said.

We looked at him sceptically. He was not even four feet tall, very thin, and perhaps ten years old.

"My name is Jose," he said, holding out his hand. Realizing what we were thinking, he added, "I don't have to grow up to be a sailor. I am one already. Don't worry, I'll sail you over at high water."

While we were waiting for the tide, Jose showed us a *maderocarril*, an incredibly simple wooden railroad that he and his father had built. Like everything else in Chiloe, it was completely fashioned by hand. The rails were hewn from split logs, the wheels carved from sections of tree trunks, and the axles meticulously rounded and greased with animal fat. The small truck resembled a mine cart and rolled easily down the makeshift tracks to the beach. Whenever one section of forest is depleted, the whole system is moved to another location. It was one of the few labor-saving devices we found.

At high tide the three of us carried the dinghy down to the shore and launched it into the river. Jose took the tiller and he suddenly changed from boy to man. Squinting slightly, he studied the wind and sails like an experienced helmsman.

"I've been sailing since I was six," he told us. "My first trip was in the summer. We went to Puerto Montt, all of us, the whole family, my sisters, my mother, and I. That was the first time I left home, the first time I saw a city, and cars, and shops; the first time for lots of things.

"We stayed there for almost a week. Dad couldn't leave the boat because he had to sell the wood, but he let my sisters and I go to town whenever we wanted to. We went everywhere.

"He promised me when I was ten I could sail with him all the time. He said he wouldn't take me before that because it gets too cold at sea. That was just an excuse. It gets cold in the house too."

"Don't you go to school?" we asked.

"My younger sisters go, but I didn't want to and Dad didn't mind. I wanted to go sailing.

"Last year Dad had to go to Quintupuepu to load some firewood. My uncle Pedro usually goes with him, but he was sick. There wasn't anyone else who could go except me.

"Quintupuepu is a funny place, sort of

"Anita"—one name for three women—a sailor's wife, daughter, and boat.

THE CHILEAN *LANCHA CHILOTA* 45

The villages are barren, continually battered by the storms of the Roaring Forties.

like a big hole in the mountain. There are lots of rocks at the entrance, but once you're inside it's nice because you can tie up right next to the shore. Nobody lives there. It's just a place to get firewood.

"Dad and Pedro had chopped all the wood the week before. We had only to stack it in the boat. That didn't take long. We finished the next day, but Dad didn't want to sail out at night. He said it was too dark to see the rocks.

"But in the morning there wasn't any wind—nor the next day or the day after. We just sat there on the boat trying to keep warm. We were stuck in that big hole.

"Why didn't you tow the boat with the dinghy?" we asked.

"Dad tried that, but he couldn't do it by himself. After three days we ate the last of the bread. We had plenty of *mate* though. Dad said if we drank enough of it we wouldn't be hungry. I drank buckets full, but I was still hungry. At low tide we rowed down to a little beach at the end and found some mussels. But that didn't fill our stomachs.

"There was a house not far away down the coast, but Dad wouldn't let me go to ask for food, and he wouldn't go and leave me alone either. I don't know what he wanted, except to get out of that hole.

Puerto Montt—the sailor's window to the world.

"Finally on Friday the launch from Puerto Montt came by. Dad rowed out and stopped it, and then they came in and towed us out. I suppose if Pedro had been there the two of them could have towed the boat out with the dinghy. I wasn't much help. But Dad never said anything to me about it."

Jose landed the dinghy alongside the old bridge abutment and we climbed ashore. On the way back across the river he tacked expertly, occasionally dipping the lee rail in the water. He knew we were watching him.

We followed the rocky beach toward a string of houses perched on the end of a bleak headland like weathered teeth on a fossilized jaw. For the next ten days we wandered from settlement to settlement, sometimes by *lancha*, but often by foot, talking to sailors and their families and trying to learn as much as we could about the lumber trade.

The weather stayed cold and overcast, a chilling, gray pall that grips southern Chile for most of the year. Some days we kept moving just to stay warm. More often than not, we slept sitting up beside someone's cookstove or huddled inside the hold of a half-loaded *lancha*.

Finally, one evening, tired and very hungry, we arrived back where we had started—Osvaldo's farmhouse. We sat around the familiar stove, our hands filled with hot bread, telling Osvaldo the news and gossip from the communities further down the coast. That night we crawled into *Anita*'s damp sheepskin berths.

The next morning Osvaldo rowed us out into the bay to wait for the *Cruz del Sur*. Rather than stop at all the settlements, the ferry slowly skirts the coast a half mile or so offshore. Anyone wishing a ride rows out and flags it down like a taxi. Afraid of missing it, we left early and spent two miserable hours bobbing in the choppy seas and getting drenched by each passing squall.

"When the weather's bad, sometimes

she doesn't come," said Osvaldo with a half smile. "Last year they stayed in Rio Negro for weeks."

We bailed the boat and didn't reply. Each time we looked up another heavy cloud seemed to be sweeping down toward us from the Andes.

Finally we heard the sound of an engine and the *Cruz del Sur* hove into sight. Minutes later, while the dinghy wallowed in the waves we somehow managed to exchange *brazos* [embraces] with Osvaldo, then climbed on board the ferry.

The cabin was overflowing with passengers and goods, huge sacks of onions and potatoes and baskets of smoked shellfish and dried seaweed. We found a place near the engine and huddled around the exhaust pipe trying to keep warm. Through the rain-soaked windows we watched Osvaldo and Chiloe continental fade into the mist.

A young woman joined us, shivering with cold and introduced herself as "Lucia from Rio Negro."

"I had a coat when we left," she explained, "but I just sold it. That's my business, selling clothes."

Like most people in southern Chile, Lucia was friendly, curious about who we were, and quite willing to talk about herself. During the long voyage to Puerto Montt we stood around the exhaust pipe and talked about life in Chiloe. Between the tales of hardship and misfortune she told us about her own struggle to survive.

"If your husband's a farmer and he dies and leaves you with five kids, you'll have to struggle to stay alive, but if you're a sailor's widow, it's almost hopeless. Man gone. Boat gone. You've got no land and nothing to sell. Who's going to feed you? Family? Yes, I suppose if you have any. I don't, not

here anyway. Friends? They disappear fast. My husband helped them a lot, worked on their boats and never charged them, but they never bothered to do much for us. Neighbors? They'll give you some flour and potatoes for a while, but if you can't give it back one way or another, they'll stop handing it out. Then what do you do? Who's left?

"Oh, the church helps some. Once a month the priest gives you a big tin of butter and some flour. You can do without the butter and trade it for something else, but that won't keep you or the kids alive. In the end you're on your own, and the kids need food and you've got no way to get it. That's what happened to me.

"One day Fernando sailed to Calbucco with a load of firewood and didn't come back. At first I didn't worry. Often it takes a couple of weeks to sell it all. Then you have to buy provisions for the next month and wait for a north wind. Three weeks went by, then I knew something was wrong. The wind came out of the north, and one by one the other *lanchas* came back. They told me he wasn't feeling well, but he was going to sail anyway. So I waited.

"Then a neighbor brought me the news. She had heard it on the radio. The boat had been washed ashore on Puluqui and they had found him dead on board. There wasn't a motor launch for a week, so Pedro sailed me over to Calbucco. It took four days to tack against that north wind, and by the time we got there he was already buried.

"So there I was. A widow at twenty-six with five small kids and no money. There are only two ways to make a living here, either cutting the logs or sailing them to

The spirit of mutual aid is still strong. One sailor's broken keel is automatically a community project.

Puerto Montt. If you don't have a man working for you, how are you going to live?"

Lucia stopped suddenly as the *Cruz del Sur* lurched off the top of a wave and began to pitch violently. We had entered the Gulf of Ancud and a high sea was running against us. Every third or fourth wave broke over the bow, sending shudders through the boat and its passengers. The

Captain tried to hold his course, but soon he had no choice but to turn, run with the waves, and seek the lee of the islands on the other side. The journey to Puerto Montt would be several hours longer, but much safer.

The cook came down the aisle, climbing over people and baggage and juggling a half-dozen bowls of hot, watery soup. This was the customary "free meal" given to

every passenger and we gratefully spooned in the warmth.

Lucia cleaned her bowl with a crust of bread, then went on, her voice softened. "I wanted to keep the *lancha.* The nicest time I ever had was when we sailed together in the summer. Those trips were like holidays. I didn't have to worry about the house or the kids. Fernando kept them busy and I had time to watch the sea and relax. I think that was the only time we never fought."

"Couldn't you sail the boat by yourself?" we asked.

"Believe me, I thought about it, for that boat kept us alive for years. My husband built it himself, next to the house, and it was like part of the family. But the oldest kids were too young to help and I knew I'd never be able to haul up that gaff boom by myself. Besides, they'd never let me do it. They'd never accept a woman. Here, no woman will ever be the *patrona* of a *lancha chilota.*

"So I sold the boat. I didn't get much for her. You never do when someone dies on board strangely like Fernando did. People think he had a pact with *Caleuche* [the devil who sails a phantom ship], or some-

thing like that, and no one wanted to buy her. Finally a merchant from Castro offered me maybe half what she was worth, but I took it. I had to.

"The money lasted for a couple of months. Then the only thing I could think of was to wash people's dirty clothes. No one likes to do it, so it wasn't hard to get the job. It wasn't really a job, just the only thing I could find.

"You see, it's always cold here near the *cordillera* and what women hate most is standing in the river, up to their knees in icy water, washing clothes. So I did it for them. I hardly had to ask. Sometimes I stood in the river all day and in the evening. I was so cold the children had to come and help me walk home. All that just for a little flour and potatoes.

"Every day I sent the kids down to the beach to collect shellfish. Then we'd string them up and smoke them. Pedro sold them for me in Puerto Montt. It wasn't much money, but every bit helped.

"The only thing I had left to sell was Fernando's clothes. And why not? They weren't doing us any good. So on Sunday, when everyone came out of church, I was there, hanging the clothes on the fence. In a few minutes they were all sold. They were good and cheap and that's what the people here need. And they didn't have to sail all the way to Puerto Montt to get them. I could have sold a lot more.

"That's how I got the idea to go into business. I took the money, went straight to Puerto Montt on the first boat, and bought more used clothes. For over two years I did that, bought and sold clothes, here and in other villages along the coast. I'd put them in a sack and carry them from place to place. Sometimes I'd get a

Without winches or blocks and tackle, all effort is measured in human terms.

ride on a *lancha*, but most of the time I walked and went from house to house. I did well, better than I expected. I sold clothes to practically everybody. They'd even come to me to ask for something special, like a wedding dress or a suit. It all grew so fast I began to save money, and for the first time the kids and I didn't have to worry about tomorrow.

"A few months ago on the way back from Puerto Montt the owner of the *Cruz del Sur* asked me if I knew someone who wanted to buy a share in her. She needed a new motor and he didn't have the money. Suddenly, I realized I had the money to do it. And I did. I gave it to him the next day.

"Now there's a boat in the family again. It's not a sailboat, of course, and it's really only half mine, but it makes more money than the old one ever did."

At dusk the *Cruz del Sur* arrived in Puerto Montt and anchored among a small fleet of *lanchas chilota*. Each boat had a sample of its cargo, a few planks, shingles or timbers, piled on its deck. The *patrons* clustered around braziers of coals, drinking *mate* and waiting for buyers to arrive. We parted from Lucia, assuring her that we would look her up in Rio Negro when we came that way again. We might be glad to buy some clothes from her.

Lumber and firewood are still very much in demand in southern Chile and the trade thrives as perhaps never before. Yet the Chilote sailor's future is a precarious one. His livelihood is fueled solely by wind and muscle, and it is only a question of time until men with power saws, tractors, and motor launches invade the islands and mechanize the industry. Then he will become as obsolete as the *caravel* on which he sails.

For the moment, however, the stormy days and seas protect him, and he accepts the rain, fog, and cold with an enviable resignation. His spirits seldom dampened, the Chilote sailor squats beside the tiller of his *lancha* as he has for centuries, exposed to the elements and seemingly accustomed to the hardship and hard weather.

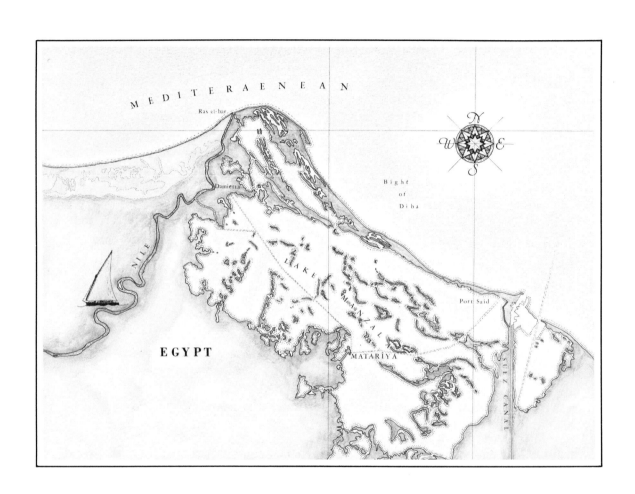

THE EGYPTIAN AIYASSA

Working sail may have made its first appearance in ancient Egypt, and today the Nile is one of its last strongholds. More than 5,000 craft—nearly half the tonnage that moves on the river—still sails upstream with the prevailing winds, then drifts down with the current, just as they have for countless centuries. One can stand almost anywhere on the banks of the river, or along one of the hundreds of canals, and within a short time the swallow wing sail of an *aiyassa* is certain to appear, the tip of its lateen yard perhaps thirty meters in the air.

Sometimes the *aiyassas* arrive in fleets of ten or more, and as one watches them sail past Giza, Memphis, or Luxor one wishes to picture in the mind's eye the way the river was in the past. But this would be a mistake. The banana-shaped Pharaonic craft have had no influence on the *aiyassas*, which are not even Egyptian in origin. Their hull form was copied from the Portuguese *galeass* and the lateen sail is thought to have been discovered in the Persian Gulf. The word *aiyassa* is actually an Arab rendering of the Portuguese *galeass*, and in Upper Egypt dialect the craft is called a *gyassa* or a *gayassa*.

Perhaps the only similarity between the *aiyassas* and the Pharaonic boats is that occasionally an eye is painted on an *aiyassa*'s bow. This custom probably began in ancient Egypt where the eye of the sun god

Ra was placed on the bows so the boat might see with the god's eyes and thus avoid danger. But whether this is a vestige of the past or merely an amulet against the power of the evil eye is a moot point.

The occulus—the eye of Ra—is the only vestige of the Pharaonic past.

Aiyassas traditionally carry bulk cargoes, mainly stone, hay, gravel, brick, and clay pots, and the center of the trade is Cairo. The port is a disorganized stretch of riverbank flanking both ends of the city, which is always dusty and never silent. We wandered along the left bank and were amazed at the intensity of activity and the density of craft. In the space of a hundred meters we found *aiyassas* being built, repaired, loaded, unloaded, hauled out, salvaged, and sunk.

We stopped to rest in the shade of a barn-sized hay rick. A bent old man hobbled over to us and motioned us toward a small brick shed. At the doorway we met Issa, a hay merchant who invited us into his cool office and poured us cup after cup of hot mint tea.

For fifty years he has been in the business, buying hay from Upper Egypt, transporting it down river on his fleet of *aiyassas* and selling it to the owners of donkey carts in Cairo. Issa looks the part of a prosperous merchant, fat and sedentary, with heavy jowls and an even heavier authoritative voice. He seldom moves from behind his tea-stained desk. Buyers, sellers, and his boatmen all come to him.

While we were in Cairo we visited him many times, and always as soon as he saw us coming he sent the old man hobbling into the kitchen to prepare tea. Like many older Egyptians, Issa has a knowledge of foreign languages and he mixes his vocabulary of French and English into a salad and speaks them as one language.

"I inherited the hay business when my father died. He left me this piece of riverfront and three *aiyassas*. Now I have eight working for me, the biggest one, one hundred twenty tons. There are two of them," he said, pointing out the open doorway toward the river. Several masts and yards were visible over the top of a haystack. "Black, yellow, and blue," he said, "those are my colors."

Nearly every *aiyassa* has its mast and yard tops banded, and each trader or owner has his own pattern. The colors, usually three or four of them, can be read like house flags or steamer funnels. If one knows the code, he can tell immediately who owns the boat.

"My *aiyassas* bring hay from upriver," Issa went on. "That's all they carry. They used to take Pepsi, beer, and rice on the return trip, but now all of that goes by train or truck so they sail back empty. It's not good business, I know, this trading in one direction, but you can't get cargoes to go upriver. And I need the hay. Sometimes ten or twelve captains get together and hire a tug to tow them upstream. That saves a lot of time, and makes everybody more money."

"Don't the boatmen ever stay in their villages?" we asked.

"No, not for long. Perhaps a day or two between trips. They're used to it, and so are their families. And maybe it all works out for the best. Who knows? It's their problem. Mine is to find sailors to keep my little fleet running. No one wants to work on my boats these days. Why should they? Eighty pounds [\$114] a month is all I can pay them. That's for the whole crew, and for that they have to load it all, drift downstream for a couple of weeks, and maybe unload it here as well. It's not easy to get men who are willing to do that. Everyone wants to run off to Kuwait, Saudi Arabia, or someplace like that where they think they can make a fortune. I can understand it. Would you sail on one of those decrepit boats?"

"Perhaps," we said, "but only for a little while."

"And work too?" Issa smiled.

"What do you mean by 'work'? Doing the loading and unloading?"

"Yes, if I can't find porters."

"We're sailors, not stevedores. You load the boat and we'll help sail her for you."

"And live on board as well? *Aiyassas* don't carry passengers and I guarantee that you won't find one to be a comfortable home. Most of them are full of rats, and don't be surprised if you meet a few at night. Just a warning—don't leave any food in your pockets when you go to sleep. Also don't take any money with you. The sailors are worse than the rats."

With a rare display of mobility, Issa got up from his desk and escorted us down to the Nile where one of his *aiyassas* was unloading hay.

We walked along the low brick fence that separated Issa's property from the wrecking yard next door. On the other side three wooden *aiyassas* were lying on the beach, their ribs naked, their masts and yards stacked ashore like telephone poles. A number of workmen were sorting through the planking, pulling out long iron nails and chopping the boards into small pieces.

"It's still good wood," Issa explained, "mango, eucalyptus, and acacia, and worth money. They'll cart it away and turn it into charcoal. Most of it ends up melting asphalt for new roads."

"What happens to the steel ones?" we asked.

"Those *aiyassas* never really die. They cut them apart and use the plates to build new ones. If you look closely, sometimes you'll find three or four generations of steel in one boat. But they're not *aiyassas* anymore. They call them *sandals,* and they all have motors. Diesel fuel is cheap here in Egypt, less than half of what you pay for it in Europe. So if you can ever get the money to buy an engine, it's not so expensive to run it."

Leaving us at the river's edge, Issa went on board a large, two-masted *aiyassa* and spoke with the *rais,* or captain. He was

Issa's opposite, thin and sallow, with sharp features and a broken nose. The *rais* gestured incredulously in our direction, and Issa replied with calming, flapping movements. After a long ballet of arm waving Issa managed to convince him that we were serious about sailing on the *aiyassa* and quite willing to work. The *rais* remained sceptical about our abilities, and from his point of view he was quite right. He'd never seen Europeans sail an *aiyassa* before, and neither had anyone else he knew. In his eyes we were untried sailors and he said so over and over. But he had little choice. Since he would be sailing with only his son Abdul, he could use the extra hands, no matter how clumsy he thought they might be.

By midday the hay was unloaded and the boat swept clean. We stood on the blistering foredeck with the *rais* and his son and worked the winch. Rusted cable wound onto the drum and we slowly raised the main yard, sail, and boom, all of which weighed the better part of a ton.

"God is one," chanted the *rais* with each half turn.

"God is Allah," replied Abdul completing the cycle.

Soon we were chanting and groaning with them, and the four of us labored for half an hour just to hoist the yard and sail into place. Then we followed the *rais* around the boat as he adjusted shrouds and backstays and explained the different sheets and halyards. Each one, we discovered, was a chaffed patchwork of knots and splices, bits of rotting line that we expected would break at any moment. When we heaved on one, we always braced ourselves should it give way, and we took the same precaution

To raise the ton or more of yard and sail is an hour's labor at the winch.

when using other gear as well. Everything from the ancient, clanking winch to the twisted hasp on the hatch was either cast off, handed down, or makeshift. The concepts of newness and permanence are unknown on board an *aiyassa*. Breakage and repair are always expected. The first time we dropped the anchor into the mud, for example, the stock broke in two. The *rais* shrugged his shoulders, as if he knew it would happen. "*Mash'Allah*," he said, "God willed it," and one could hardly argue with that. He threw the pieces into

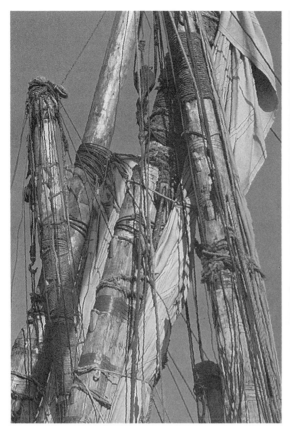

No part of the rigging ever arrives "new." Everything is pieced and patched, an ever-changing pattern of rope and chain.

the hold on top of a pile of broken blocks and fittings that eventually would be sold, traded, or welded into some new device.

We hoisted sail, first the main and then the *mazzaan*, or mizzen, the word being Arabic in origin. The huge sails caught the wind instantly and we glided out into the river. Abdul spread some rags and tattered pieces of sailcloth on the shady portion of the deck and that became our quarters for the voyage. We ate and slept there, and as Issa predicted at night the rats came to fight over any bits of bread that might

have fallen onto the deck. After the first few nights we learned to live and sleep, so to speak, with them.

The *rais* sat astride the tiller, and ordered Abdul to prepare tea.

"To become a sailor you have to begin as a cook," he told us. "Everybody starts that way. At first, you just make tea, fill the captain's waterpipe, and try to stay out of everyone's way. The next thing you learn is how to climb the yards and reef the sails. The mizzen is easy. It's not so high. But when you're only eleven or

"Later my father taught me the Nile. As we sailed he told me, 'Go here, not there, look at the color of the water, it's only ten hands deep, there fifteen, watch the wind at the bend, take the curve close to the mosque. And don't forget,' he always told me, 'the most dangerous thing is not the river, but the riverboats. No matter what anyone says, they always have the right of way.'

"Two years ago my brother was killed by one of those steamers. His *aiyassa* was loaded with brick, overloaded really. They had less than a hand of freeboard. 'Sailing with your coffin' is what we call it. They were coming to Cairo one night when a steamer hit them. It ran right over them. The *aiyassa* sank straight away. The two crew swam to shore. But my brother was below. He never had a chance.

"When we were boys, for years we worked the tiller together, he on one side, me on the other. It takes a lot of force to steer an *aiyassa*. When the day comes that you can do it alone, then you become a boatman. Here, try it. You'll find out for yourselves."

The tiller was over three meters long and nearly as thick as the mizzen mast. Some sacks and bits of sheepskin had been tied to the end to form a cushion and one leans or sits on it. Despite the long leverage, the rudder is difficult to turn and you must brace your feet against slats nailed to the deck and push with all your strength and weight. Maneuvering an *aiyassa* is like a strenuous workout in a gym. Nearly every muscle is called into play. To go from full port to full starboard, the helmsman must push or pull the tiller across the entire beam of the boat.

Other *aiyassas* drifted past, going down-

twelve and you look up that main yard for the first time, you don't want to leave the deck. I certainly didn't. There are steps all right, but they're not close together, not for a boy's legs. So you have to hang on to whatever your hand can find, a sail hoop, rope, or just a crack or a lashing. The first few times my father had to beat me before I would scramble up. But once you get to know the mast, going up it is as easy as walking across the deck.

Fully loaded, an aiyassa *has only a few inches of freeboard.*

The port of Cairo is jammed with craft awaiting salvage and rebirth.

stream stern first, broadside, whichever way the current took them. Clearly, they had the right of way and we weaved among them.

"Come have tea," one captain shouted as we passed by, giving the traditional greeting among boatmen.

"*You* come have tea," our *rais* replied.

"Where did you get the tourists?"

"They're supposed to be sailors," our *rais* laughed. "But they can't make proper tea and won't climb the yard."

We turned to avoid another oncoming boat and the captain's reply was lost on the wind.

The *rais* took the tiller and ordered us to haul in the block and tackle attached to the end of the main yard. The Helwan Bridge was now less than half a kilometer upstream and one way or another we were going to pass beneath it. We pulled the yard down, pivoting it on the masthead until it was horizontal and the canvas hung like that of a square sail. We pivoted the mizzen yard as well. The tallest part of the boat was now the top of the main mast.

"How high is it?" we asked.

"About fourteen *deraas* ['arms'—measured from the tip of the nose to the end of the fingers]," the *rais* replied.

"And the bridge?"

"About fourteen *deraas*."

"About?"

"More or less."

As we drew closer we could see it was going to be a tight fit. But the *rais* seemed unconcerned. He calmly sat astride the tiller, his feet wedged against the slats, his eyes half closed. At the last instant he glanced up at the trestle, altered course and chose a place on the span where one I-beam seemed to be slightly higher than the rest. He lined up the *aiyassa* and we watched the mast top gently scrape the steel and pass between two rows of rivets.

"That was a bit risky," we said.

"No," smiled the *rais*, "not at all. I know all the *aiyassas* on the river. The one that passed ahead of us has a mast the same height as mine."

The moment we cleared the bridge we started to pivot the main yard aloft. It was half raised when the blocks jammed. The *rais* immediately sent Abdul scrambling up the mast, but by the time he had picked out the bits of chafe that filled the sheave, it was too late. The boat lost way, then the current caught us, swept us around, and sent us crashing bow first into a thick patch of reeds. The wind filled the sail, driving us in deeper, and the tall reeds closed over us like the flaps of a tent. From a distance only the mast and yards would have been visible, and it must have looked as if the *aiyassa* had sunk into a green reedy sea.

The four of us quickly furled the sail,

a tiny fluke that inhabits a species of snail. At a certain point in its development, the fluke leaves the snail and searches for another host, which it enters through the skin. Thus, one can drink Nile water without fear of catching bilharzia, but one can't bathe in it.

The captain looked up at us expectantly, wondering why we weren't in the water helping him. We hurriedly tried to decide what to do. The flukes often take some time to work their way into the pores, and if one washes well after being in the river, they can usually be rinsed off. But wash with what? The only water available was that from the Nile.

then Abdul and the *rais* jumped over the side into the chest-deep water and began to push on the bow.

We hesitated to join them. The Nile, especially the slow-moving waters such as those along the banks or in reeds or swamps, is a vehicle for bilharzia, a debilitating disease that infects over half the Egyptian peasantry. Although it can be deadly, more typically bilharzia leaves its victims functioning at only half their capabilities. We often noticed that boatmen seemed to lack stamina, and since the river is their water supply, undoubtedly most of them are infected. The disease is passed by

Fortunately, the decision was made for us. Another *aiyassa* had been a few hundred meters behind us, and seeing us go into the reeds, altered course to pass by our stern. The crew shouted and held out a towrope. We ran aft to take it, and quickly made it fast to the mizzen mast.

The *aiyassa* luffed her sails until the line was taut, then with surprisingly little effort pulled us stern first out of the reeds. Abdul and the *rais* climbed on board, dripping with slime. The *aiyassa* luffed her sails again, while we carried the towrope forward to the main mast. In a few minutes we were in the middle of the river with the wind aft. The *rais* took the tiller, and we lowered the booms to set the sails.

The four of us waved our thanks to the other boat, but it was neither necessary nor expected. Mutual aid is one of the laws of the river.

Once underway and past the bridges of

Cairo there was little work to be done on board. We quickly settled into a slow, quiet routine. One man steered until he got tired or bored, while the others lay on the deck and slept or smoked. Abdul made tea whenever anyone requested it.

We sailed all night without lights or a lookout. "The wind comes with the darkness," the boatmen often say, and despite the hazards most of them prefer to sail at night. Occasionally we overtook another *aiyassa*, drew alongside to exchange greetings, then immediately sheered off. By some unwritten rule, an *aiyassa* is always given at least two boat lengths of sailing room.

On the second night the *rais* entrusted the boat to us. "Keep your eyes up," he cautioned. "Watch out for black triangles. The bigger they are, the nearer they are. Stay close to the bank and away from motorboats." Then he wrapped himself in a bit of old sail and slept till dawn.

With a steady breeze and a straight, wide river we could hardly make a mistake. One leans against the tiller cushion and dozes lightly, glancing up every few minutes at the dark river. The unmuffled exhaust of the steamers could be heard a half mile away, and since they ran with lights it was easy to stay clear of them.

We left Abdul and the *rais* at Beni Suef, where they were to take on a cargo of lime-

Each repair is a fresh problem, a new solution to a puzzle of knots and splices.

The hull form came from medieval Europe, wide in the bows, narrow in the stern.

Patching the huge sail is a daily chore.

A rais or captain, with his master's license.

Even though the *aiyassa* population still numbers thousands, it is a quarter of what it was fifty years ago, and diminishing rapidly. In the salvage yards of Cairo, every day sails come down that will never be hoisted aloft again. But in an odd twist of circumstances the reason for the *aiyassa*'s demise is not just the usual one, that of motors replacing sails. In addition, and probably more important, is the fact that the goods that *aiyassas* transport are passing out of use. The traditional cargoes are either no longer in demand or being replaced by modern products. As the number of donkey carts decreases in Cairo, less hay is sold, aluminum pots are taking the place of clay, and since the Aswan dam has curbed the yearly flood, the brick industry is running out of silt and will soon cease to exist. In a few years there will be very little left for the *aiyassas* to transport.

"The trade is dying, I know that," Issa once told us. "The time is coming when I won't need so much hay. Then I'll sell two or three of my boats and build a gas station by the road. That way I can't lose. Whatever comes along, a donkey or a truck, I can feed them both."

But one *rais* with whom we sailed was not so sanguine or pragmatic about the future. "In the old days before an *aiyassa* made her maiden voyage the captain took his knife and drove it deep into her stem to kill any evil that might be on board. Now whatever they launch is made from steel. There is evil in every one of those boats."

stone, then by boat and train we made our way up the Nile to El Minya, Qena, and Balas. Finally an *aiyassa* put us ashore at Luxor nearly in front of the temple of Karnak. We had followed the Blue Nile for almost all of its navigable length and we had seen, we guessed, nearly 500 *aiyassas*.

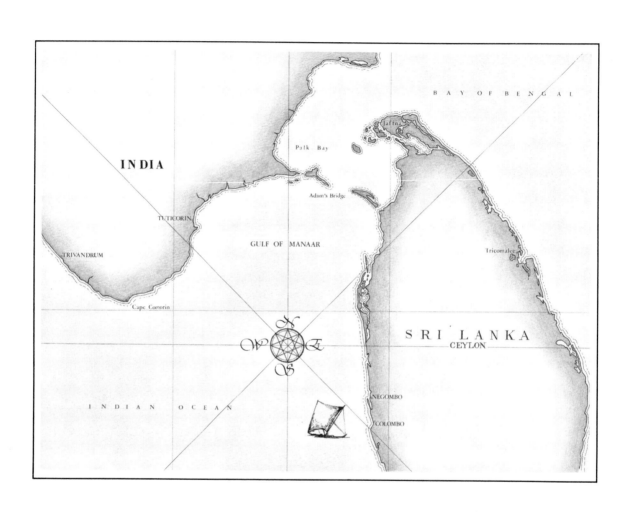

THE SRI LANKAN
ORUWA

We sat on a bamboo platform lashed between the two outrigger booms and watched Stanley, the captain of the *oruwa*, prepare to come about. He loosened a bit of frayed line that held the steering oar in place, then nodded to his father, who was at the other end of the dugout. The canoe was cutting across the seas at more than eight knots so the timing would have to be perfect. The slightest error would leave us windless and ready to broach to on the next big wave.

"*Arul marukaramu* [Ready about]!" Stanley shouted.

The two crew quickly passed the sheets and the sail through the V of the two masts, and at the same moment, Stanley raised his steering oar and his father lowered his, then secured the sheets. The *oruwa* neither gybed nor came up into the wind. It simply lost way, stopped, bobbed in the waves for a few seconds, then the wind caught the sail and it began to move in the opposite direction. The tack of the sail had become the clew, and the clew, the tack, and, of course, the stern was now the bow, and the bow, the stern.

For Stanley, this is all quite normal. *Oruwas* are meant to sail in both directions. When we explained how our sailboats came about, he only laughed. "Why do you make the ends of your boat different? Put the mast in the middle. Look how well it works for us."

It was difficult to argue the point.

Although an *oruwa* has the unique ability to sail ferrylike, backward and forward, the craft does, in fact, have a bow and a stern. The dugout canoe that forms the lower part of the hull is hewn from a single tree. The lower and fatter part of the trunk is called the bow and the tapered end, the stern. Which way does an *oruwa* sail best? Stern first or bow first? We asked Stanley and other fishermen if they had a preference, and they always replied with a slightly puzzled expression, as if to say, "If we hadn't wanted it to sail both ways we wouldn't have built it like that."

Perhaps the most remarkable feature of the *oruwa* is its method of construction. Except for a half-dozen brass bolts used as twarts, the various pieces of the craft are either lashed or sewn together. The *oruwa* shipwright literally threads a needle and, stitch by stitch, assembles his boat. To join the two parts of the hull, the washboards and the dugout canoe, holes are drilled along the edges, the seam covered with coconut matting, then the pieces sewn together by means of a simple cross-stitch. The punt-shaped bow and stern projections and the gunwale beading are also sewn. A thick coat of black gum provides waterproofing. Originally coir rope was used as thread, but recently this has been replaced by inexpensive nylon line. Hand-twisted

All seams are sewn, coated with tar, covered with split bamboo, and held in place with coir rope.

Reinforced with branches and lashed into a tight bundle, the outrigger support is as strong as steel.

coir rope is still used, however, for the lashings that bind the outrigger to its booms and the booms to the hull.

The practice of sewing ships together is an old one. The Pharaonic craft of ancient Egypt were sewn ships as were the *dhows* of the Arabian Gulf and India. Where and how this method began is a mystery, but the Sri Lankan *oruwa* is certainly one of the last survivors.

But despite its timeless appearance, the *oruwa* is a comparatively recent craft. According to oral tradition, it first appeared about 150 years ago. Before that time fishing along the Ceylonese coast was confined to lagoons where men netted prawns from small dugout canoes. Later the prawns were used as bait and the fishermen ventured out to sea. The canoes became longer and their sides were built up with washboards for protection against the sea and surf. The sail is said to have originated when a fisherman hung his *sarong* between two oars and discovered that the wind could drive his canoe faster than any man could hope to paddle. The oars grew into masts, and the *sarong* into a large rectangular sail. The last refinement was the heavy steering oar that was added about a century ago to give the craft a semblance of a keel.

Oruwas can now be found along the entire west coast of Sri Lanka and the greatest concentration of craft is at Negumbo, a small town that fronts both the sea and a large, shallow lagoon. Fishing has always been the main industry there, and the quiet waters of the lagoon serve as a harbor for several hundred craft. They sit on chocks just a few inches above the water, row after row of sewn ships, each one an exact copy of the next.

Like workboats in many other parts of the world, *oruwas* are regarded as tools and seldom given names and personalities. When Stanley first gave us directions to find his boat, he said, "It's the third *oruwa* after you cross the bridge."

"Doesn't it have a name?" we asked.

"Sometimes people call it 'the fish buyer's boat' since he owns it."

These informal names are usually taken from the owner's profession, his title, or perhaps the name of his business. We were told that if, for example, we were to own an *oruwa*, undoubtedly it would be called, "the European boat."

Depending upon the season, *oruwas* trawl for prawns several miles offshore or troll further out for seerfish, a member of the mackerel family, whose tasty flesh brings a high price. We arrived during the prawn season and quickly found ourselves at sea, sailing *oruwa*-style backward and forward combing the muddy bottom with a dragnet.

At the end of each sweep we lined up with the crew in the narrow hull and hauled in the net, which was weighted with two fifty-pound slabs of iron. At first Stanley's father sang and we pulled in rhythm hand over hand, but as the sun rose higher the singing stopped and we all groaned and panted instead. Getting the weights on board was always a frantic maneuver that usually ended with someone's fingers twisted in the lines. Too often they were ours, and by the time we had mastered the simple but elusive skill of hauling in the net without losing a single prawn our hands were battered and blistered.

Stanley, the *thanndal*, or captain of our *oruwa*, was a curious mixture of cultures and typical of most fishermen along the coast. Sri Lankan by birth, he rarely uses the national language but prefers Tamil, the language of his forefathers who immigrated from southern India. Although Sri Lanka is predominately Buddhist, Stanley is a devout Catholic and always gives a twentieth share of his catch to the Church.

Endowed with a short, chunky body, on

board the *oruwa* he was as agile and light-footed as a dancer. His frown was fearful, but we soon learned that there was always a smile behind it, and his good nature seemed to have no limits. When another *oruwa* sailed across our wake and fouled our net, the crew shouted abuse, but Stanley merely saluted the other captain, shrugged his shoulders, and cut the tangled lines. A few days later his nephew, a boy of fourteen, accidentally dropped a full basket of prawns, half the day's catch, in the water. Stanley silenced the crew and said quietly, "It can't hurt to feed the fish."

To keep himself and his parents alive, Stanley fishes six days a week and his working day is often twelve to fourteen hours. His pleasures are few, and those one would expect of any sailor—women and drink. A stiff shot of coconut arrack, or toddy, or perhaps two or three, is the customary way to end the day, and the women of the port have adapted themselves to his odd hours.

That morning, for example, he woke us at 4:00 A.M. The three of us walked through the darkened streets stopping in front of each crew member's house. "Eeeee-ay," Stanley called out, and a few seconds later a reply came from within. On the edge of the lagoon we passed a dimly lit thatch hut. Two women were squatting in the doorway, and whistled quietly at us through their teeth.

"You get the net and sails from the shed," Stanley told us, "and I'll meet you at the boat."

We loaded the boat in the growing dawn, and around us were the shadows and voices of other men preparing their *oruwas* for a day at sea. The rest of the crew arrived and helped us push the boat off the chocks and into the water. Stanley jumped

Mast down, the oruwa *can be easily poled or paddled.*

on board, then we slowly poled our way toward the mouth of the lagoon.

"Who were those women?" we asked as we raised the sail.

"Twilight girls," he replied.

We looked puzzled.

"They work in the twilight, in the mornings before the fishermen leave."

"And in the evenings too?"

"Sometimes," he said, "if the catch is good and we have money."

At sea, the method of fishing was always the same, a kind of crisscross sailing that soon became a familiar, practiced routine. We tacked upwind as far as possible, lowered the net and paid out the lines, one from the stern and the other from the end of the outrigger. Then we shifted the sail to the other end of the boat and using the full force of the wind, dragged the net for perhaps half a kilometer. If the wind died or suddenly veered, we manned the oars.

After each sweep the catch was dumped on the platform and we sat cross-legged in the middle of it sorting the fish into one basket, prawns into another. Shells, rubbish, and seaweed went over the side and all spines and spikes seemed to end up in our fingers. We didn't like the work and said so.

Stanley agreed with us and climbed out on the platform to give us a hand. "Fortunately, we only go fishing for prawns a couple of months a year," he said. "Too bad you're not here in the spring. Then we go out twelve, fifteen miles and troll for seerfish. You have to move fast, as fast as an *oruwa* will go, ten knots, maybe more. There's plenty of wind out there. Lots of waves. Sometimes so much spray is flying about you don't have to wet the sail. It's soaked halfway up. An *oruwa*'s built for that, catching seerfish, and no motorboat can beat us. When you get one on the hook, they fight hard, and you have to pull with all your force, sometimes two, three of us together, to get them on board. That's real fishing. All we do here is scrape the bottom."

"If the weather gets bad, how do you reef the sail?" we asked.

"What do you mean 'reef'?"

"Make the sail smaller."

"We don't. We either leave it up or pull it down completely. An *oruwa* can take a lot of wind."

"Do they ever capsize?"

"It happens, but not often. Last year a boat near us went over. It was blowing hard and two men were sitting on the outrigger. That's what we call a 'two-man wind.'"

In Sri Lankan terms, a "one-man wind" is already a stiff breeze, and a "four-man wind" approaches a full gale. Contrary to what one might first think, the log that forms the outrigger (usually a jackfruit or breadfruit tree) is not used for buoyancy, but rather as a counterpoise, or counterweight against the force of the sail. Hence, an *oruwa* always sails with its outrigger to windward. As the wind increases, more weight is added. The outrigger also serves as a kind of liferaft. If the boat capsizes, the fishermen can always cut the coir lash-

ings and at least have a float to cling to.

"They were trying to take down the sail," Stanley went on, "but they waited too long. A wave hit them broadside and over they went. We picked up the men all right, but there wasn't much we could do about the boat. One of the booms was broken and so were the masts. You can't right an *oruwa* at sea, even when it's calm. We cut off the outrigger and towed it and the hull back to shore. By the time we got there it was too late to sell the catch, so we just gave it away. It doesn't matter, though. Someday I may need a tow."

"What happens if you're at sea alone?" we asked.

"More than likely you'll have to leave the hull. The best thing is to make a *tepam* [raft] out of the outrigger, booms, and masts and then sail or paddle back as best you can."

"Do *oruwas* ever get lost?"

"Sometimes. But we lose more men than boats. Once somebody goes into the water it's difficult to find them. My brother Antony fell overboard last summer. It was a bad day and they shouldn't have gone out at all. Most of the other boats stayed in the lagoon. I did too. They were out there all by themselves. It was simple. It always is when an accident like that happens. A wave broke over them. Antony was at the steering oar and when the boat came out of the water he was gone.

"They bailed out the boat and went back for him, but, of course, they didn't know where to look. They sailed in circles till dark. After that there wasn't much point, so they came home.

"Antony was still alive. He said he often saw the sail of his boat from the top of a wave, and just before dark he watched them turn and sail away. You can imagine how he felt, alone out there in bad weather, maybe ten miles from shore. The next morning he was almost at the end of his strength when he swam into the remains of a fishing net. That was luck and saved his life. He ripped out a couple of the floats, lashed them together, and tied them around his chest. Then he began to swim. I'm not sure if I would have made it. No water, no food. The sea calmed down, so that helped some. After three days he reached the shore further down the coast. You should have seen the surprised faces when he got off the bus in the Negumbo market."

At noon we heaved to. "*Ele aleawanawa* [siesta time]," Stanley proclaimed as he brought the *oruwa* up into the wind and adjusted the sail so that it shaded most of the boat. We lay down on the platform, sharing the space with the two crew, while Stanley balanced himself on the gunwales and used the mast step for a pillow. The only person left in the sun was Stanley's father, who tied a bit of cloth around his head as a kerchief, and dozed lightly at the helm, occasionally giving the steering oar a kick to hold the boat in position.

The rest of the fleet followed our lead and soon within less than a square kilometer of sea upward of 300 men were sprawled across their boats taking a nap.

We slept for about an hour, then Stanley's father turned the boat and let the sun wake us up. Once again we untangled the lines and net and threw the weights overboard. After three short drags the wind suddenly veered onshore. The entire fleet turned as if a single hand controlled all the tillers and like a nautical ballet a hundred sails headed toward home.

We entered the lagoon and joined twenty other *oruwas* already nosed onto a sand spit in front of a tin-roofed shed called "the auction market." The fish buyers were waiting on the beach. Most are *mudalali*, "middle men" or "sharks" depending on how the word is used. They often own several *oruwas* and are always the first ones to come on board and inspect the catch.

Vincent, the *mudalali* of our boat, stood at the water's edge. Wearing pants instead of the customary *sarong* and a well-pressed white shirt, he seemed completely out of place among the crowd of children and fisherwomen, like a banker who had just arrived at the seaside for a holiday.

"I hope you've worked hard," he said to us as he poked through the baskets of prawns trying to judge the value of the catch. Doesn't look too bad. Perhaps I'll hire you two for another day."

"You'll have to pay us for today first," we replied.

"Why?" he said. "It was good experience for you."

"Is this what you call experience," we said, holding out our bruised hands. "We worked, now pay us."

"Don't worry," he said, "you'll have plenty of prawns to eat tonight."

After the catch was sold and the money divided, we helped Stanley and the crew pull the *oruwa* onto its chocks and wash it down with sand and water to clean off any marine insects. *Oruwas* are never painted, but once a week, generally on Sundays, they are given a protective coat of coconut oil.

We had dinner with Vincent at his home, a spacious stone house facing the sea, and, as he promised, the main course was prawns, cooked Sri Lankan fashion in a rich spicy curry. We cooled our mouths with toddy, a lightly alcoholic wine made from the flower of the coconut palm, which is the fisherman's favorite drink. While we ate we asked Vincent how the *mudalali* system worked.

"I take half the catch," he explained, "and they split up the rest among themselves."

"Can they live on that?" we asked.

"Yes, just. They take life day by day. Nobody thinks much about the future, which is, I suppose, why none of them owns their own *oruwa*. Somebody has to buy one for them to work on."

"Like you?"

"It's an investment like any other business. A new boat costs about twelve thousand rupees [about $850]. That's half the price of a fiberglass launch, so if you don't get fifty percent of the catch it's not worth doing. On a good day, like today, we all make money, on a bad day we lose. And me more than them, of course. Today we sold the catch for two hundred rupees [$8.00]. That's about average, I guess. I know they take a little extra sometimes, in fact, most of the time, but I don't mind as long as it goes to their families."

"Don't they want to have their own boats?"

"I'm sure they would say 'yes' if you asked. But in any case it's impossible. They never save anything. If they make twenty rupees [80¢], they spend it. If they make one hundred [$8.00], it also goes straight to the market. They'll buy something, more rice, cloth, or just toddy. You can be certain by the time the evening is over all the money will be gone. The idea of saving, for months or years, to buy a boat has never occurred to them. And they won't go into partnership either, which is the sensi-

ble way to do it. They're just not businessmen.

"They're a strange lot. Money doesn't mean much to them. Not yet, anyway. Sometimes they even give a day's work away. You see, when someone dies or gets married they don't even have enough money to have a party for their friends. They're that poor. So the community helps them. Word goes around that on such and such a day everyone will go fishing to pay for a funeral or a marriage. The whole day's catch, that of maybe a hundred boats, goes to the family, and it could be thousands of rupees. If the family is lucky, there'll be plenty left over after paying all the expenses. Ask Stanley about it. When his brother Antony got married there was enough left to buy a new bicycle. It's an old custom and no one knows quite where it came from."

Our dinner was interrupted by the noisy arrival of Vincent's cousin, Fernando, on his new motorcycle. Like Vincent, Fernando has done well by the sea. Although only in his late twenties, he already owns three fiberglass launches, two of which he runs as a *mudalali*, and the third he uses himself.

Several days later we went fishing with him in his nineteen-foot launch. On the way back from the fishing grounds he promised to weave through the *oruwa* fleet so that we could take some pictures.

We motored out seven or eight miles, cast the gill net, and were soon hauling in large quantities of fish. In the distance, further down the coast, the *oruwas* were hull down. Only their large, rectangular sails were visible, looking like a pack of cards spread out over the horizon.

"They're not very clever people," Fernando said. "They fish all day, and what do they make? Twenty rupees [$1.00], thirty? I can make ten times that. I have to pay for fuel for the outboard, but I'm still

In front of the market the oruwas *dry their sails.*

better off. And they know it. They're jealous too. As long as they don't have the money to buy a motorboat they say they don't want one. We've always had trouble with the *orucarayo* [*oruwa* fishermen], right from the beginning. About fifteen years ago, when we first started to use motors, they were afraid we'd steal all the fish. They burned some of our boats and cut our nets. Every evening there were fights in the auction market. It's all settled now. They fish in their grounds, and we in ours."

Later we talked to a local lawyer and discovered the reason for the hostility. When motorboats first began to fish offshore, they dumped enormous quantities of fish on the

market, and, of course, prices fell dramatically. They didn't steal the *orucarayo*'s catch, just augmented it. The low prices were no great handicap for the motorized fisherman, who made up for it in quantity, but for the *oruwa* fisherman, who lives day to day and suddenly found his income cut by half, the introduction of motorboats was a disaster. Quite logically, he struck out against them. Fistfights in the market grew into organized raids to destroy the fiberglass boats. The motorized fishermen defended themselves and soon a minor war was raging. The dispute ended up in the courts where the judgment went against the *orucarayo*. The seas are free, the court ruled, and open to anyone who wants to fish. The number of motorboats increased and the Negumbo fishing community has remained divided ever since.

The launch loaded with fish, we motored into the middle of the *oruwa* fleet and began to take pictures while Fernando weaved around the boats being careful to avoid their trailing lines and nets.

Suddenly, the engine spluttered and died. The three of us took turns pulling on the starting cord, but the motor refused to even cough.

"Sand in the carburetor," Fernando said.

A search through the boat produced only a rusted screwdriver.

We looked helplessly at one another for a few moments, then Fernando reluctantly took the split bamboo pole that served as an oar and held it aloft as a signal of distress.

A large *oruwa* changed course and sailed toward us. Standing in the bow, holding a coiled line, was Stanley.

"Don't worry," he shouted as he threw it to us. "I'll sail you home."

The *oruwa* easily towed us back to Negumbo. Fernando didn't say a word, but sat glumly in the stern enduring the humiliation of being towed through the lagoon by an *oruwa.*

"That wasn't the first motorboat I've towed in," Stanley told us later. "They're always getting into trouble. If something breaks they don't know how to fix it.

Motors are too complicated. They should sell them all and buy *oruwas.*"

And that, in fact, may be slowly occurring. There are now more *oruwas* sailing from Negumbo than ever before. The rising cost of fuel has altered the vision of the future, and the fisherman's dream of standing at the wheel of a powerful motor launch is fading rapidly. To lure men away from diesel engines and outboard motors, the Sri Lankan government now pays seventy-five percent of the cost of each new sail, and boatyards that produce fiberglass launches are beginning to experiment with fiberglass *oruwas.* Progress is looking backward, and the traditional is gradually becoming the modern. Once again, the lagoon of Negumbo is crowded with sailing craft.

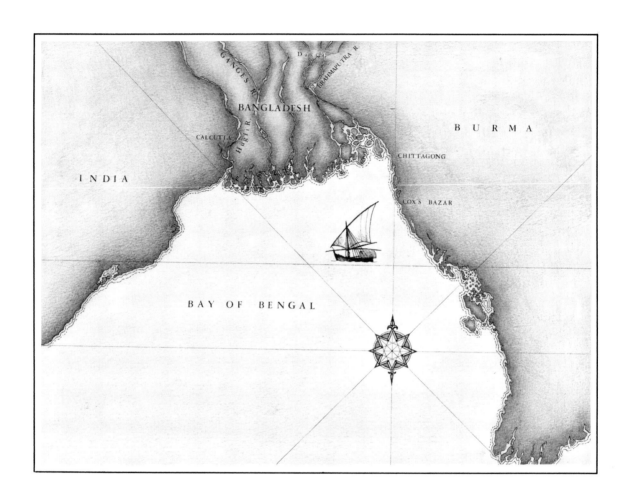

THE BANGLADESHI
SHAMPAN

From the air, Bangladesh appears to be a huge delta, a country of islands, clumps of green rice fields wedged between the fingers of the Ganges, Brahmaputra, and the Jamura. These and dozens of other rivers and their tributaries form what is perhaps the most complete system of inland navigation in the world. Rivers flow to and from nearly every corner of the country, and on them, sails by the thousand, cast like grains of rice across the country's muddy veins.

These are sails of every shape and description: junk sails, square sails, spritsails, Bermudian sails, and lateen sails, a mixture of Asia, Europe, and the Middle East. No one knows how many boats are in the country. Guesses are always in the hundreds of thousands, and if one were to count all the dugout canoes, punts, and lesser craft, the total might well approach a million.

Most are riverboats, endlessly ferrying people and goods from bank to bank, stream to river, and river to headwaters. But in the southern part of the country, along the panhandle that juts into Burma, one finds larger craft—huge, lumbering ships that transport salt, dried fish, and rice across the treacherous Bay of Bengal.

These are the *shampans,* whose high, squat sterns make them ideal for carrying bulk cargoes. The *shampan* is of Chinese origin, but over the centuries the Bengalis have remade it into a boat of their own.

The junk sails have been replaced by the more familiar lateen rig, and the hull rounded and flattened so that it can be beached anywhere.

The southern coast of Bangladesh is an even, intricate web of rice paddies, cut by innumerable rivers and creeks. Behind them rows of gentle hills fade into the blue Burmese mountains.

We traveled in an ancient jeep left over from the Second World War, sharing it with no less than ten other passengers and a half-dozen sacks of rice. The road ran along the tops of the dykes and weaved around the paddy fields as though it were following the lines of a checkerboard. It ended abruptly at the head of a muddy creek. Four empty *shampans* rode high in the water waiting for the tide to turn.

The captains were taking tea ashore under a lean-to made from cast-off mats. We were invited to join them and quickly learned that all four boats were bound for the island of Kutubdia, which was our destination as well. Kutubdia supplies much of the country's salt and the *shampans* would stay there for several weeks loading their cargoes. We spent the afternoon in the shade of the lean-to, and after the third cup of tea one of the captains agreed to take us.

When the tide ebbed, we helped cast off the lines and poled the *shampan* down the creek. A feeble, offshore wind filled the

Like giant ducks, the shampans *are often carried with the tide.*

sails, but lacked the force to drive the ship. As soon as we reached the sea, the crew broke out four long pointed oars, stripped off their shirts, and began to row from the foredeck with short deep strokes.

We joined the other *shampans* who were rowing as well, and like a fleet of galleys, the boats glided across the quiet water. The Bay of Bengal appeared to be serene and harmless.

"Don't get the wrong idea about the Bay," said the *maji* or captain. "What you see now is only one face. The other has the eye of a cyclone." Sitting cross-legged on a bamboo mat, he held the tiller with one hand and chain-smoked with the other. He was the smallest man on board, gaunt and so thin that whenever he ate a bowl of rice we were sure we could see the difference. Between cigarettes, he stroked his beard, which was cut in the customary Moslem style, shaved upper lip and well-trimmed cheeks.

Like most sailors we met in Bangladesh, the *maji* had a cyclone story to tell. Every few years a revolving storm whips across the Bay of Bengal and ravages the southern part of the country, devastating rice paddies and consuming hundreds of craft and thousands of lives. There are few places in the world where one encounters so many sailors with so many tales of heavy weather and shipwreck.

"The cyclone of '70 was one of the worst," the *maji* began. "I was a sailor then, working on a *shampan* carrying salt to Chittagong. The storm caught us at sea, about ten miles off the coast, not far from here. There was no warning, none of the usual signs. Suddenly, the sky turned black and it began to rain. It came down like waves from the sea. The sails were ripped to shreds before we could take them down. We all dropped to our knees and asked Allah to save us, but the wind was so strong it blew away our prayers. The *shampan* lay on her side. Water ran over the deck. Lightning was everywhere. The captain made us cut down the mast, but it didn't make any difference. The storm took us with it. We all knew what was going to happen and we just hung on to whatever we could and waited. Every *shampan* in the Bay was in the same state. No one escaped that cyclone.

"When we struck bottom, the *shampan* died. She rode up on a wave, then smashed onto the ground and cracked in two like an egg. And just that fast too. I fell into the water and so did everyone else, I think. A few minutes later I saw two of my friends holding onto the rudder. I swam toward them, but they were swept away into the night, and that was the last I ever saw of them. I never saw any of the others either, or the boat. I think it sank straightaway.

"For maybe four or five hours the waves carried me with them, and it was all I

could do to keep my head above water. I had no idea where I was until my legs brushed against the branches of a *kerfa* tree. Then I knew I had to be near the shore, but the water was so high my feet couldn't touch the bottom. I grabbed hold of the branches and wrapped my legs around the trunk. The waves went over me, all angry and full of foam, and sometimes I held my breath so long I thought my chest would explode.

"Then, all of a sudden, the current changed and the tide began to run out into the Bay. It was like a torrent, coming down from the mountains. It bubbled around me and broke my grip on the tree. Just when I was sure I couldn't hold on any longer and would soon join my friends who were swept out to sea, I felt something grab me from behind. Whatever it was, it took hold of my *longi* [sarong] and held me there like a stake driven into the ground. I was too frightened to turn around. I thought perhaps it was the hand of God, and Allah had decided it was not my turn to die. Or maybe it was *Khwaz-Pir* [a sea god in the form of a dervish] awakened by the storm. I didn't know. I was only thankful that the water rushed past me and I didn't go with it."

The *maji* paused to light another cigarette and leave his listeners hanging for a few moments. We still had a long way to go to Kutubdia, so he was in no hurry to finish his story. Besides, a good yarn is always a long one.

"Finally I got enough courage to let go of the branches with one hand," he continued, "and reach behind me. My fingers crept along the top of my *longi* and I didn't know what to expect. Then my hand closed on another. I turned my head but it was so dark I couldn't see who or what it was. I tried to shout against the wind, but it was useless. I reached further and felt the body of a man, and when I put my face to his, I knew who it was. Our captain. I embraced him, and for the rest of the night we stood there, our arms around each other and the *kerfa* tree.

"At dawn we saw another *shampan* not far away. It was lying upside down and a man was on top of it. The current had slackened a little, and going from tree to tree, we made our way to it and climbed on board. Like us, the sailor had lost the rest of his crew. All that day and the next night we clung to the boat. The tide raced in, churning around us, but the wreck didn't move. When the tide went out, it carried with it all kinds of debris, roofs, broken boats, and the dead bodies of people and animals. The following day the storm began to subside and at low water we waded ashore and found a country boat that was stranded on a dyke. We bailed it out, climbed in, and paddled to higher ground.

"The captain's village was not far away, so I went there with him. Nothing was left. You hardly knew there had been a village, just scars on the mud where the houses had been. The captain lost his whole family, wife, children, parents, everyone. I took him home with me. He went back to sea, of course, but I wasn't surprised when he disappeared in the next cyclone."

As we looked out at the windless sea, and the flat ribbon of our wake, it was difficult to imagine a cyclone's violence. The Bay of Bengal seemed as tranquil as a lagoon.

The crew were still rowing, their backs

now wet with sweat. Occasionally, one of the oarsmen sang, and often the song was picked up by the others, but no one marked time, for to do so brings bad luck to the ship. Like any other craft, the *shampan* has its own special catalog of taboos and omens. One must not play cards or gamble at sea, climb on board with shoes or sandals on, and after raising the anchor a symbolic bucket of water is always sloshed over the prow. On Thursdays one shouldn't sail south, on Saturdays and Mondays, east, and on the fourteenth day after the full moon, one shouldn't sail at all.

Ahead of us, the long, low profile of Kutubdia grew on the horizon. The island is little more than a maze of rice paddies whose highest point is only a few meters above sea level. A dilapidated jetty called the *Steemir Ghat* (steamer landing) marked a small market community and we beached the *shampan* beside it. One of the crew swam a line to shore and tied it to a piling. A few hours later the tide went out, leaving the *shampan* aground, sitting upright like a fat duck on the mud.

We jumped over the side and found ourselves knee deep in black ooze. Struggling to keep our balance, we had just begun to wade toward firm ground when behind us we heard a cry as the cook, an elderly man with a wispy, Chinese beard, slipped on the bulwarks and fell off the boat. He

landed badly with his arm outstretched. Covered with mud, he lay in the slime, writhing and clutching his shoulder. His arm had come out of joint.

The cook is usually an old man or a young boy and paid the least of anyone on board. Our cook never helped with the sailing of the ship. His only duty was to boil the rice on an open fire, and prepare any fish that were caught.

We rushed over to him, sliding across the mud as though it were mushy ice. His face had turned white and he made little effort to hide the pain. We helped him stand up, then guided him to shore. In the market we washed the mud off him and ourselves. The captain joined us, then we hired two rickshaws and set out to find the local doctor.

He was sitting on the veranda of his office engrossed in a well-thumbed thriller. As it turned out, there was little for him to do. A recent graduate, he had been posted to the island by the government, but given few drugs to administer. Any serious cases were sent by boat to Chittagong. Frustrated by his lack of supplies, most of the time he sat and read and waited for emergencies like ours.

After a quick examination the doctor deftly slipped the cook's arm back into joint. The old man sighed heavily as the pain eased, then gratefully downed a few ounces of "medicinal" alcohol. When he regained his strength, the captain helped him back to the boat. We stayed behind to talk to the doctor.

The three of us went back to the veranda and settled into ancient long-sleeve chairs.

"If that sailor's arm had been badly broken, I'm not sure what I could have done for him," the doctor said. "As it is he won't be able to work for a couple of weeks and I don't know how he's going to stay alive. We can't feed him here. The owner of the *shampan* won't help him. I'm certain of that. Hopefully his family will be able to take care of him, but one never knows. Next week he might be sleeping in a ditch. If he does, he won't be alone. You see, most people on this island are poor and landless. Perhaps they own a little hut, but they still have to pay rent for the land. Where are they going to get the money? Working in the rice fields? That only employs some of them. Kutubdia is like the rest of the country—there are too few jobs and too many people. For many men the only way out is to become a sailor. Don't think they want to. People here have few illusions about the sea. You've seen what it's like to work on a *shampan*, and that's not the worst of it either. Forty boats went down in the last monsoon, and more the year before. The Bay of Bengal is a graveyard, and every one of those sailors knows it."

"Do *shampans* ever get lost?" we asked.

"Not really. The tide sets north and south, and the sun moves east to west. There's your compass. It's the storms that do them in. *Shampans* are fine in good weather, but during the monsoon the Bay is so rough not even the navy goes out of port. But the *shampans* sail. They have to. If they don't work, the crew starve, and almost everyone in Bangladesh has sampled that horror."

Contrary to popular opinion, the monsoon is not a storm, but a season, three or four months of rain beginning in May. In Bengali it is called *Kal Baisakhi*, "the disasters of May," and as much as twenty inches of rain has been known to fall in a single storm.

"Don't waste your time painting any romantic pictures about iron men braving the seas," the doctor continued. "If they don't sail, they don't eat. No more, no less. And on board they do whatever the *maji* tells them. He's like a little god who sits there at the tiller. You'll never see him touch a rope or an oar. When he says load the boat, they do it, wading through the mud with maybe twenty or thirty kilos of salt on their heads. It can take weeks to fill up a boat like that. And when there's no wind, they row, eight or ten of them at the oars, sometimes all the way across the Bay, twenty-four hours or more. How they manage to do it all day I don't know. The strange thing is they're glad to have the work, and when they sing, you almost think they don't feel the misery."

"How do you know so much about the *shampans?*" we asked.

"My father owned three of them and I'll never forget what it was like on board. Working on one of those boats is the closest thing to slavery I know. All that effort and toil, for what? Two or three hundred *hakas* a month [about $8.00 to $12.00]? That's barely enough to keep a man in rice, much less feed his family. And suppose he breaks something, or loses it overboard—a rope, a block, it doesn't matter what—the owner will charge him for it. And the full price too. He may have to work months to pay it off. A sailor is lucky if he can just exist and keep his stomach full. When he needs more money, say to fix his house or marry off a daughter, then he's in trouble. Maybe he can get an advance from the owner of the *shampan*, but probably not. He usually ends up in the

pocket of the moneylenders. Then he's really finished. They'll charge him whatever they can, ten percent, twenty, twenty-five. He's illiterate and doesn't know what he's signing, much less how to compute the interest. That's the monthly rates, by the way, so it doesn't take long before the amount he owes is an impossible sum, many times the original debt. The moneylenders will feed on him for years. Everything he makes will go to them.

"I suppose you think I'm being cynical," he said, seeing that we were slightly incredulous. "But I assure you I'm not. I've known these people all my life, and I can tell you that anywhere a sailor looks some-

thing or somebody is waiting to prey on him, and I don't mean just the monsoons and the moneylenders. Bangladesh is a few centuries behind the times. What may be history for you is often the present for us. It may not look like it, but the Bay of Bengal is a frontier, like in one of your Western movies. Last week I had a sailor in here with a bullet in his arm."

"Who shot him?"

"Pirates, I guess. He didn't say."

"What do you mean, 'pirates'?"

"Dacoits, thieves, perhaps not as romantic as Blackbeard or Captain Kidd, but pirates just the same."

We asked the doctor how we could find the sailor and he gave us the name of the man's village, a small salt port several kilometers down the beach.

After talking to a number of sailors we discovered that pirates are a fact of life in the Bay of Bengal and the *shampans* and fishermen have learned to live with them and, if possible, elude them. There are, of course, no doubloons or pieces of eight to be captured. Modern booty is more prosaic—the catch and nylon nets of fishermen or a *shampan* cargo of rice, dried fish, or salt.

The pirates usually go out in rowboats or motor launches and pose as fishermen several miles offshore. When a likely victim is near, two or three men set the nets and pretend to fish while the others hide beneath the sail. If the pirates can get as close as 100 meters before they are discovered, the prize is theirs. An eight-oared longboat can easily overhaul a heavily loaded *shampan* even when it is sailing with a favorable wind.

Their weapons are simple, the age-old cutlass and crude, homemade pistols. According to those who have had the misfortune to meet them, the pirates are still as bloodthirsty as legend would have it. Strange as it may seem, the one-eyed corsair still scrambles up the chain plates with a sword in his teeth.

The next morning while the crew began to load our *shampan* with salt, we set out to find the wounded sailor. Following the coast, we walked along the crest of a low dyke and had the strange illusion that the sea and land were reversed. Inland, green wind waves rippled across the rice paddies, while seaward, the tide was out, and vacant, black mud flats reached to the horizon. Every few kilometers we passed a concrete storm shelter on stilts, a grim reminder that at will the sea can rise and sweep across the island.

We found the sailor easily. The village had only one tea shop, and he was installed in the middle of it, telling and retelling his story to a small group of sailors. Two more listeners were welcome arrivals.

"That's what they did to me," he said, pointing to his bandaged arm. "Two shots." He winced, but obviously more for effect than from pain. "Everyone wanted to give up the minute the boat came alongside. Why should they fight? It wasn't their *shampan*. It wasn't their rice. But I had a new pressure lamp on board and I knew the pirates would take it. I grabbed an oar and hit the first one who climbed over the rail and knocked him into the water. Then two more jumped on board. I hit one in the stomach with the end of the oar, but the other grabbed me from behind. We went down on the deck, kicking and wrestling. I screamed at my friends to help me, and finally they began to fight. We might have beaten them, but they had guns. As soon as I saw one pointed at me, I stopped fighting. I yelled at him not to shoot, but he did anyway. Twice. After that, we all gave up. They put us in their rowboat and took the *shampan*.

"I'm not the only one who has fought with the pirates," he said, turning to the sailor beside him. "Show them, Nurul."

The man pulled up his *longi* to reveal a large, ugly scar that creased his thigh. "It was after the big cyclone, ten years ago," he explained. "We had supplies from the Red Cross on board and we were taking them out to the islands. We passed a small country boat, just a dugout, with five or six men in it. They waved and shouted they were sinking, so we went alongside. Like Abdul, we thought they were fishermen in trouble. That's what I got for it," he said, pointing to his scar. "One of them cut me with his sword."

"Where do the pirates come from?" we asked.

"Cox's Bazaar, the islands, almost anywhere along the coast. But you would never know them if you saw them. They act like poor fishermen and hide their boats in the small creeks."

The pirates are not alone in the backwaters. A large population of smugglers share their refuge. Of course, smugglers can also be pirates, and pirates, smugglers, and apparently quite often the two prey on one another.

The smugglers trade with Burma. The border is officially sealed, but the sea lanes

Left: The huge flat transom was copied from European craft, and the balanced rudder from the Chinese.

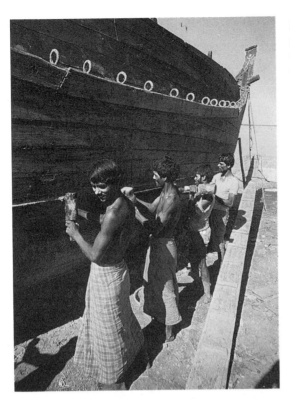

Left: The eyelets are chain plates that distribute the strain of the mast along the entire length of the hull.

Below: The crude tar acts as a kind of anti-fouling for the hull and wards off marine insects.

are only lightly patrolled. A large *shampan* can easily take on a cargo of sugar and cigarettes in Chittagong or Cox's Bazaar, head out to sea, then at night slip into a small port on the Arakanese coast. Cloth, tobacco, leather goods, and gold, which is substantially cheaper in Burma, make up the cargo for the return voyage.

On the way back to the *Steemir Ghat* we stopped to watch four men construct a *shampan* on the mud flats. There are few boatyards in the country, so most new craft are built, like this one, on the mud near the high-water mark. Four times a year the rivers flood and automatically launch whatever might be on their banks. Knowing their deadline was approaching, the men worked quickly, and if necessary, they told us, at night by torchlight.

The large U-shaped transom had already been built and was propped in place with bamboo poles, as was the hewn stem. Like constructing a box, the men were joining the two ends of the boat with planking. One board was laid on top of the next, edge to edge. Small triangular slits were cut in the top board and nails driven in them at right angles to the seam into the next plank. Then the slits were plugged with wooden chips. The wood, we noticed, was all well used, salvaged from previous *shampans* and riddled with nail holes. Many of the boards, especially those of teak, looked as if they had migrated through several boat lives.

Only when the hull is finished, literally a shell like an empty vessel, will the frames and floors be added, each one individually tailored to fit. This is, of course, the opposite method from that used in the West, where a skeleton of keel and frames is built first and the planking screwed or nailed on

afterward. But working from the skin inward is without question the older method. Some of man's first craft were built in this fashion, the planking pegged or sewn. Frames and floors were added later for reinforcement when ships began to venture out onto the high seas.

The idea of constructing the skeleton first seems to have originated in Europe, probably in the fourteenth or fifteenth century, and was then exported to the rest of the world. Somehow, the *shampans* have clung to the original method, and the craft the four men were working on in front of us would be remarkably similar to those built by their forefathers hundreds, if not thousands, of years ago. For them, the boat is still the shell, the skin that keeps out the sea, and what we regard as the bones, the essential spine, merely a necessary afterthought.

We stayed for nearly a week at the *Steemir Ghat* and when it became obvious that our *shampan* would not be fully loaded for some time, we joined another boat bound for Chittagong. The *shampan* was an old one, a twenty-year veteran of the seas, and she creaked and groaned alarmingly with every passing wave. "One more voyage, perhaps two," commented the cook, as he watched us poke the timbers. Rot fell out like dandruff.

Below, we could see the planking work with the wave motion, shifting laterally as though they had come adrift from their fastenings. Whether the ship would finish this voyage was a question; that it would not make another one was a certainty.

The *maji* seemed unconcerned. He sat erect, staring at the horizon, while the crew engaged in the traditional pastime of sail-

A simple method to make a slipway—beach the boat, then dig out the riverbank.

ors who are not at work. They found comfortable bits of deck in the shade of the sail and went to sleep. The *maji* roused them only when he wished to come about, for a *shampan* usually must be rowed from one tack onto the other.

With a convenient, following wind, we entered the mouth of the Karnaphuli River that forms the port of Chittagong. Ahead of us a deeply laden freighter was anchored in midstream unloading coal. A dozen or

more small *shampans* were nested around her, serving as lighters and shuttling back and forth to a depot a quarter of a mile away. Passing alongside one of the loaded *shampans*, we watched the crew throw large lumps of coal overboard.

We turned to the *maji* for an explanation, but he only smiled and waved an index finger that the subject was not to be discussed.

Later we learned that unloading coal is a

THE BANGLADESHI *SHAMPAN*   99

lucrative business for the *shampans*. They are paid by the ton—the tons they receive from the freighter, not the tons they unload at the depot. On the way to the jetty they throw as many lumps as they can into the river. After the freighter has sailed, they return to the spot, anchor there, and dive to retrieve the coal.

The port was jammed with small craft, rafted sometimes six and seven deep against the quay, and nearly all of them powered by either sails or oars. The diesel engine and the outboard motor are still exceptions rather than the rule, luxuries few can afford, for Bangladesh is one of the poorest, if not the poorest, country in the world. Wind and muscle are among her only resources. One port official told us, "If the world's oil wells were to dry up tomorrow, people and goods in Bangladesh would still move from place to place just as they always have."

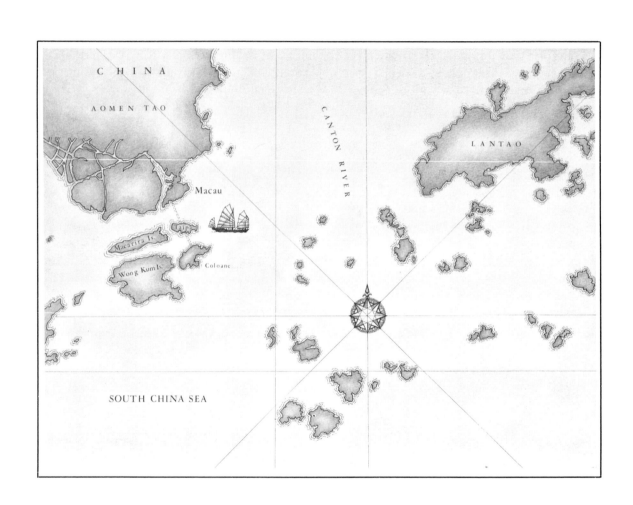

THE CHINESE JUNK

Awkward and cumbersome to the European eye, the Chinese junk seems an odd craft to meet the seas. Its sails look fragile and irregular and its blunt shape lacks a hydrodynamic form. The bow is too low, the stern too high, and the transom too broad. Yet no other sailing craft has endured so long. For the entire span of recorded history, at least five thousand years, the junk has remained basically unchanged.

While Europeans were paddling skin coracles and making their first experiments with oceangoing craft, the Chinese were building huge junks that carried tons of cargo and hundreds of passengers. They had already developed the compass, the stern rudder, watertight compartments and perfected the junk-rigged sail. In 100-meter, nine-masted ships, Chinese merchants voyaged throughout Southeast Asia and sent expeditions to Arabia and the east African coast. Had a fleet of these enormous junks reached the Mediterranean, no doubt Europeans would have regarded them with much the same awe as American Indians did when they first saw the Spanish caravelles and galleons. But by the time Europeans arrived in the Far East, China had lost interest in a maritime empire, turned inward, and nearly severed contact with the outside world. The huge trading junk had become extinct.

The Portuguese were the first to settle permanently on the Chinese coast, and for over four centuries they have maintained the tiny colony of Macau at the mouth of the Pearl River. No bigger than central London, Macau is still an *entrepôt*, a way station between China and the West, and, as always, many of the cargoes arrive and depart in the holds of junks.

The word "junk," we discovered, is a recent invention, a term of convenience, coined by Europeans, that includes virtually all the sailing craft of the China Sea. More than likely it comes from the Javanese *djong*, meaning boat or ship, which became *junco* in Portuguese, then *jonk* in Dutch. In fact, there are dozens of junk types, each one as different from the next as a sloop from a schooner. The Chinese sailor seldom uses the word. Instead, he calls his craft by the local name that is usually the port or river where it was originally built. In Macau, the most common junk is the *Tam Kok Teng*, that is, the *Teng*, or "boat" of Tam Kok, a small port on the Pearl River.

Like workboats in many other parts of the world, junks are rarely given distinctive names. They are regarded as tools and homes, mobile implements that are devoid of personality. If one needs to distinguish one junk from the next, he calls it by the captain's name, "Lee's *Teng*," or "Wong's," but not the *Sea Dragon* or *The Evil Eye* as popular belief would have it.

We spent one afternoon on a Portuguese police launch patrolling the watery frontier with China. Illegal immigrants, "I-I's," as they are called, constantly try to slip into Macau by sampan and junk and the Portuguese authorities make an effort to turn them back. We stopped and searched several suspicious craft but found only cargoes of rice and dried fish. Late in the afternoon the boatswain suddenly pointed toward the tip of Ma Lo, the nearest Chinese island. A junk with a large mud-colored sail was tacking toward us.

The captain looked through his binoculars. "Boat people," he exclaimed, and began to maneuver the launch as close as he dared to Chinese waters.

Although the seas were slight, the junk was having difficulty making way. It rode deep in the water and from a distance almost seemed to sink behind each wave. As it drew near we counted the heads and waving arms—thirty-four people—about three times the number one expected to find on a ten-meter craft. They had sailed over 600 miles, much of it across the stormy Gulf of Tonkin, and the rest battling the erratic winds of the south China coast—not an easy voyage under the best of conditions.

We looked at them through the binoculars, and hundreds of photographs flashed before us—humanity at its worst: exhausted, enfeebled, and famished. The boat people were war's leftovers, cast adrift to fend for themselves and hopefully reach a friendly port.

Their junk was crude and worn, a drab, unpainted gray, splotched with rusted nail heads, and quite unlike the finely crafted boats made in Macau. It leaked so badly that three or four men bailed constantly.

"Hong Kong? . . . Macau? . . . Hong Kong?" several people shouted at once, pointing to the red and green flag on the launch's stern.

The captain called the United Nations office by radio, then stepped out on deck to assure the refugees that their journey was over.

As the junk came alongside we were smothered by a terrible stench, a putrid odor one recognizes instinctively. In the bottom of the hold was a rough, newly made coffin. The junk lowered its sails, then we towed it to the police jetty and tied it up to leeward. Within minutes the entire harbor knew there was a dead man on board.

While we were waiting for the UN officials to arrive, we talked to the Vietnamese captain, Tran van Loc, a civil engineer. He sat on the landing, gripping the concrete steps to steady himself as though he were still at sea.

"We had no illusions from the beginning," he said, "from the moment we decided to leave. Lots of stories have come

back to Vietnam, so we knew it wouldn't be easy. But we never expected it to turn out as it did.

"My uncle," he pointed to an elderly man clad in the traditional black pajamas, "found the boat and captain, and the others to share the cost. It took weeks to arrange. Finally we all met in a tiny village south of Danang. Some fishermen let us use their huts. We had to pay them, of course, but they were kind people and gave us a good meal before we left.

"About midnight, in two's and three's, we crept down the beach and waded out to the boat. My uncle had bribed the village guard, but we had to be careful just the same.

"The first day was terrible. Nearly everyone was seasick. The old people were the worst. They lay in the bottom of the boat and moaned and pleaded with the captain to turn back. For most of them it was their first time at sea. I guess they thought the boat would be bigger, with cabins and perhaps an engine. It was a bit of a shock. When they looked over the side the water

up the ladder she slipped and fell overboard.

"We turned around, but it took a long
time. The boat was so full you couldn't
make any maneuver quickly, not even
lower the sail." Tran gestured toward the
junk's waterline, which was green with
algae. Amidships, there was less than half a
meter of freeboard. "We couldn't find her.
We looked all morning, everyone stood
and searched, but there wasn't a trace. The
moment I heard her scream and looked up
to see her fall into the sea I knew she was
lost. She couldn't swim.

"After that, the elders had a big discussion about whether or not we should turn
back, but it was just talk. We had a lot of
trouble with the captain too, right from
the beginning. He promised everyone there
would only be twenty people on the boat,
but when we left there were thirty-seven of
us. There wasn't even enough room for us
all to lie down at the same time. We had
to take turns sleeping.

"The farther we got from Vietnam, the
worse he became. All he thought about
was money. Money for water, money for
rice, money for everything. We'd already
paid him for the food, but he thought he
owned it and made us pay again. If we
didn't, he threatened to put us ashore. He
knew everyone had a little gold or jewelry
with them, and little by little he tried to
get it. He nearly did too.

"Except one morning he wasn't at the
tiller, and my cousin, Lee, was lying unconscious in the bottom of the boat with a
big cut on his forehead. There was nothing
we could do for Lee. He died the next day.

"I was the only one who had sailed before, so the elders made me the captain. It
was a long time ago, when I was a boy, but

was only inches away. Every time a wave
lifted us they thought the boat would turn
over and sink.

"It was hot, a kind of heavy heat you
don't find ashore, and the sail gave us only
a little shade. They started to see things—
patrol boats and airplanes, even soldiers
and demons. They were afraid of the sea,
afraid of the land, afraid of everything.
You can't blame them. In Vietnam people
have learned how to be afraid.

"On the third day we lost my sister.
There was a toilet on the stern, just a few
boards and a piece of cloth in front of it. It
had rained all night, and when she climbed

once I took the tiller, it all slowly came back to me. The first thing I did was change course toward Hainan island so we could bury Lee."

"Why didn't you bury him at sea?" we asked.

Tran looked at us quizzically as though the question made no sense. We learned later that a watery grave is an unthinkable horror for a Chinese sailor. Unable to join his ancestors, his spirit is condemned to perpetual limbo. It is still the custom among the Chinese that when a body is found at sea, it is always taken on board, then buried ashore. If the person's identity remains unknown, a small statue representing him is placed in the family shrine that is found on board every junk. The drowned sailor, symbolically at least, becomes a part of the junk's family and his destiny is fused with theirs.

"Three days later," Tran continued, "we saw Hainan and the next evening we sailed

Every sailor is represented in the ship's shrine.

into a small port and anchored near the quay. But the Chinese wouldn't let us land. A police boat came alongside and told us to go on to Hong Kong. We showed them Lee's body, and begged them to take it, but they wouldn't. The other junks wouldn't take it either. The next morning we traded a watch and some rings for a coffin, then the police towed us out to sea.

"We kept to the coast and whenever the weather looked bad we found a bay or harbor and dropped anchor. The fishermen were good to us, and always showed us the way to Hong Kong. I suppose they knew we had things to trade. But no one ever let us go ashore. For over two months we lived on that little boat."

Several buses arrived at the head of the jetty and the refugees began to move toward them. Tran got up to leave. His junk had already begun to fill with water and only Lee's coffin remained on board, lying across the stern like a silent epitaph.

We joined the Portuguese sailors and helped carry some small children and be-

longings to the buses, then came back for the coffin. The UN officials counted heads, signed a receipt, and formally took charge of the refugees.

"They were lucky," the Portuguese captain remarked as we watched the buses leave for the resettlement camp. "For every five or six boats that escape from Vietnam, the Vietnamese patrols get one, the pirates another, and a third, or maybe even a fourth is lost at sea. How many, no one will ever know for sure."

We left the police jetty and walked along the waterfront of Macau's Inner Harbor, a congested tangle of piers, godowns, and rafted fishing boats. The dockside streets were full of stevedores unloading cargoes of rice and animals from China, fish from Hainan, and manufactured goods from Hong Kong. In the gaps between boats, or under their bows or sterns, market women sculled their sampans, floating bars, shops, and restaurants. The waterfront is like a city within a city, one that seems to thrive on activity and seldom sleeps. Day or night, as soon as one boat leaves the quay another moored midstream quickly takes its place.

The largest craft in the harbor is one that never goes to sea—a red, ornate, three-storied barge called the *Macau*

In every port the sampan *is the dinghy, lighter, and ferry.*

Floating Palace. Unlike the other casinos that cater to the tourists, the *Floating Palace* tries to satisfy the gambling needs of the waterfront, especially those of the sailors and fishermen who have a reputation for being inveterate gamblers. It is often said that the fishermen of Macau don't fish to live, rather they fish to gamble.

Inside the *Floating Palace* the gambling halls are unpretentious, no plush carpets or glittering chandeliers, just rows of fan-tan, blackjack, and high-low tables that are open twenty-four hours a day.

We joined a crowd clustered around a game of high-low, which is one of the fishermen's favorites. Three dice are thrown, and one bets either high, eleven to seventeen, low, four to ten, or for higher odds on the number or exact combination that will fall.

We stayed with the low numbers and after a short run of luck we began to lose steadily. The man next to us, however, had a good winning streak, and we noticed that he always seemed to bet in the opposite manner from us. If we put money on high, he took low.

As we were about to leave the table we asked him, "Why did you always bet against us?"

"Somebody has to win," he replied, cashing in his chips. "Tonight was my turn, tomorrow, yours . . . well, maybe. We'll see tomorrow. Anyway, I'll buy the drinks."

We left the casino, crossed the street, and sat down in a noisy sidewalk food stall. Above our heads a radio blared a Chinese opera, and at odd moments drums rolled and cymbals crashed.

The gambler was Chu Li, the captain of a sailing junk that plies between Hong Kong and Macau. He lives on board with his family, wife, two sons, infant daughter, and grandparents. Once a week, his junk brings general cargo to Macau, then returns to Hong Kong loaded with blue jeans and T-shirts manufactured in Macau, but labeled "made in U.S.A." Chu has sailed all his life, making a living in whatever way he can, fishing, trading, or transporting goods and contraband. We later deduced that he occasionally takes part in the huge illicit trade with China.

Fishermen and sailors are the only people who come and go from the mainland as they please. They have always done so, and many of them carry three sets of papers—one Chinese, one British, a third Portuguese, and all of them legal. The situation obviously breeds smuggling and the profits are enormous. China is starving for the goods of Hong Kong, especially television sets and electronic gadgets, and there are still many people in China who would pay a fortune to be put ashore at night in Hong Kong or Macau. The subject is seldom discussed mainly because most of the smuggling is controlled by the Triad, the Chinese version of the mafia.

"Of course, they sell their fish here and get a good price for them too, but what they really want to do is double or triple their money, or perhaps put it all on one number and hope they'll never have to fish again. But as you found out for yourselves, that doesn't happen often. A night or two in the *Floating Palace,* then they go back to sea with empty holds and empty pockets."

"Do they gamble at sea as well?"

"No, never," Chu replied emphatically. "The crew of a junk is usually a family, and it's not right to take money from your brother or uncle. When we're in port, it's another matter. There, you can always find people to gamble with. Whenever you see three or four junks tied together you can be sure there is a game going on. One of the children usually sits on deck to watch out for the police. Gambling's forbidden in China, you know, and if you're caught you may spend a long time in a labor camp. Macau is the only place where you don't have to worry."

At dawn the next day we helped Chu hoist sail.

The halyard winch is a simple affair, a trunk of hardwood slung between two uprights and turned by half a dozen stout spokes. One uses both hands and feet, climbing the spokes as though they were a ladder. Chu's two sons joined us, and with five pairs of straining arms and legs we slowly raised the heavy canvas.

Almost instantly the wind caught the sail and we pivoted on our anchor. We ran forward to a similar winch in the bow, and hauled in the anchor as we gathered way and sailed over it.

The junk sail is one of the most efficient man has ever devised. Stiff, fairly flat and very closely controlled, it has an aerodynamic virtue that was not fully appreciated until science began to explore the behavior of aerofoils. The Chinese claim it resembles a human ear that is "always listening for the wind."

The secret of the sail's efficiency lies in the bamboo battens that serve a number of functions. In addition to keeping the sail in the proper shape so that it can be finely trimmed, they simplify the process of reefing and enable the sail to be doused rapidly. To reef, one eases the halyard and lets

the sail fall into the lazy lines formed by the topping lifts. As the sheet becomes slack, the wind automatically spills from the sail, and when enough reefs have been taken, the sail is set up again by tightening the mainsheet. It is said that one man can take three reefs in as many seconds even on the largest of junks.

Since the battens also provide support, weaker and cheaper sailcloth can be spread, and a junk sail can have half its surface full of holes and still be drawing well. Should the boat sink, the sail can be taken down, tied into a roll, and used as a liferaft the crew can cling to.

The number of battens to each sail

The windlass is crude, yet embodies the essence of mechanical advantage.

least, make a symbolic acknowledgment that at will Tin Hau can intervene with their destiny.

Chu chose the latter form and at the mouth of the harbor he turned the junk to face the temple of Ma Kok Miu and let the boat kowtow to the shrine. His sons set off strings of firecrackers on the bow to frighten away the demons, then we all took stacks of fake banknotes and threw them into the sea. The denominations were huge, tens or hundreds of millions. The more generous the offering to Tin Hau, the more care and good fortune she will return.

"Tin Hau fights the storms," Chu explained as he dropped a fistful of bogus dollars into the water. "Sometimes she comes and quietens the seas by surfing through them on a straw mat or she traps the wind with her words. They say that once in the middle of a typhoon she drew a whole fleet of junks to safety by only her will.

"Don't be so sceptical," he warned. "The gods have known the seas far longer than we have. Sometimes they come to help, sometimes not. They have their own reasons. When they arrive, you know it. If a bird lands on top of the mast during a storm, that is Tin Hau who will protect you from the seas."

The junk's wake was littered with billions of dollars. Whether or not Tin Hau realized that they were just crudely printed, recycled paper was a question we did not ask.

We pulled in the mainsheet, and once again the heavy junk quickly gathered way. Chu stood on the aft deck holding the steering lines like reins. The harbor was full of traffic, fishermen arriving and departing, and cargo boats jockeying for posi-

varies greatly. In general, the further north one goes in China, the more battens per sail one finds. The junks of Canton have the least number, from four to six, while those of the Yangtze sometimes carry as many as forty.

Our departure from Macau coincided with the festival of Tin Hau, a legendary maiden who controls the fate of men at sea. Nearly every junk on the Chinese coast takes note of the date, the twenty-third day of the third moon. The crews go ashore to worship in a temple, prepare offerings of food or money, or at the very

Ribbed with battens, the junk sail draws the wind long after a Western sail would be in ribbons.

tion along the quay. Junks passed us port to port and port to starboard, whichever way they liked. There were no rules. Yet somehow Chu seemed to sense which side the oncoming boat preferred, and he deftly maneuvered his way through the crowded anchorage.

Unlike Western craft, a junk is steered by lines that are lashed to the end of the tiller and run through two sets of blocks and tackle, one fixed to the starboard bulwarks, the other to port. For a sailor accustomed to a wheel or tiller, it's a little like driving on the wrong side of the road. Everything is reversed. Instead of pushing on the tiller, one pulls in the line in the

opposite direction. Letting us steer the junk was a constant source of amusement to Chu and his family.

Five miles past the breakwater we watched the horizon gradually disappear into the sea. The mouth of the Pearl River seemed to close over us, leaving the junk becalmed in an ominous, gray fog.

Chu filled a water pipe made from a thick piece of bamboo, took several puffs, then spat over the side.

"You asked me yesterday why I gave up fishing, well, you saw the answer in the harbor. All the junks have motors now. They don't worry about the wind; they go wherever they like and use the mast to

The foresail is cut from cotton, but the mainsail is woven from reeds.

hold up the TV antenna. I could do the same, I suppose. I should, I guess. That's what my sons want: a motor and electricity for their radios. But I like the wind. It wouldn't be the same sailing without all the little noises it makes against the sail or whistling through the deadeyes. I'd hate to have a motor going bang, bang, bang, all day and all night.

"About the time the other junks were putting in engines business really started in Macau. Shops and little factories were everywhere and they were all making clothing as fast as they could and sending it off to Hong Kong. For a while there weren't enough boats. The shipping agents were running up and down the waterfront looking for anyone to take the goods away. It was a better business than fishing, less work too. So I sold my nets and used the money to fix up the boat. A junk full of fish or a hold full of blue jeans, it doesn't make any difference to me."

The hold below us where the jeans were stored is divided into watertight compartments whose space is sold like containers. A shipper rents a section of the hold, then crams as much merchandise as he can into it.

The transverse bulkheads that form these compartments are the real foundation of the boat. A junk was traditionally built without a keel or stern post and it is the bulkheads, including those that form the transom bow and stern, that bear the strain. During the maritime era the larger, trading junks had longitudinal bulkheads as well, something that eluded the Western mind until the nineteenth century.

Suddenly, we heard the shrill clap of a Chinese gong, but as often happens in fog it was difficult to locate the source.

"Another boat in the mist," Chu explained, as he sent one of his sons forward with a winch spoke to beat a reply on the hull.

We peered into the mist, looking for the dim outline of a junk, but none appeared. The fog became thick and patchy, making distance difficult to sense. Chu stood up and quietly paced the deck. For the next half an hour no one said a word.

"They were close," he said, as he sat down on the taffrail, "no more than three boat lengths away." His wife brought us a pot of tea. "Before you finish two cups," he went on, "the fog will lift."

"How can you be so sure?"

"After thirty years at sea one knows the signs. Look over the side, there, at your reflection. See how it shimmers, and seems to glisten. The mist will be gone soon.

"Sometimes the sea changes before the sky," he continued. "It may be a beautiful day, with a south wind and a few clouds, but the sea can feel a storm coming and tells it to the fishermen. As soon as they begin to catch crabs and sea urchins in their nets, they know the weather will change, and not for the better. The old people say that the sea sings a warning before a storm, like the tingling of little bells, but I've never heard it myself. I only know that when the wind turns north and there is lightning to the east it's almost too late to run for port. Nowadays, of course, you don't have to watch anything, the sky or the sea. Even the smallest sampan has a transistor radio and can listen to the storm warnings from Hong Kong."

"But suppose you are caught in a storm, then what?" we asked. "How does a junk prepare for bad weather?"

"First, you try to get as far out to sea as you can," he said, giving us a lesson, "the

further, the better—away from the islands
and the other boats. Use all the sail and go
as quickly as you can. The sea will save
you, not the land. That's the most important thing to remember. Some sailors think
they can get into port quickly and tie up
before the storm hits. Maybe they can, but
to try it is a good way to lose your boat.

"As the wind gets stronger, you reef the
mizzen and when the sail is completely
down, if you can, lower the mast as well
and lash it down on deck.

"Next, you start reefing the mainsail and
the foresail at the same time, dropping
them one batten at a time, until you take
them down too.

"A sea anchor helps sometimes, rope or
nets running from the bow or stern.
Where, depends on the boat and the
waves, of course. Some people put their
gold and jewelry in the nets as well and
hope that the sea will take them and spare
the ship. After that, there is nothing else to
do. The sails are down. The sea anchors
are out. The tiller is lashed. The wind and
waves will take you where they wish."

Unlike the Western sailor who often tries
to dominate the sea, the Chinese sailor
tends to react passively, adopting a neutral,
accepting role as if to propitiate the sea.
To some extent the design of the junk is a
logical outcome of this mentality. Strong
and watertight, if given enough sea room,
it will fend for itself and float through almost any storm. Thousands of years ago
Lao-Tse set the course: "The way is like a
boat that drifts."

The mist lifted gradually, like a changing series of filters, and by nightfall the sky
was clear and we could see the glow of
Hong Kong.

The next day with a following wind we
entered the harbor, the only sailing ship in
sight. The narrow channel between Kow-
loon and Victoria was filled with craft and
we bounced over their wakes as though
crossing a confused sea. The *Star Ferry*
screamed at us with its whistle, then
passed close to our stern. A dozen tourists
pointed their cameras toward us and captured a classic photo: an old, lumbering
junk with tattered sails silhouetted against
the steel and concrete horizon.

Chu brought the junk up into the wind,

then let her drift slowly against the quay. His son jumped ashore with the mooring lines.

Chu's shipping agent, Sam Wong, was on the quay to greet us. He collected the manifest and after we cleared immigration and customs, we went with him for the customary cup of tea. The small room in the back of an electronics factory that doubled as his home and office was full of nautical things, ships' models, paintings, carvings, and glasswork, most of them broken and all of them covered with layers of dust.

It is easy to glean the impression that the Chinese love the sea and their boats for, as a theme, junks are ubiquitous. They appear at the head of menus, sail in fleets across fabrics and wallpaper, serve as props for advertisements, and have become an endless source of inspiration for jewelry and trinkets. No Chinese restaurant is complete without a picture of a junk bound for the horizon, its sails darkened by the sunset.

But the originals, the classical junks that have existed for millennia, are disappearing rapidly.

"There are no sailing junks registered in Hong Kong," Sam told us, "not one. Those few you do see in the harbor come from China. But don't think people miss them. They hardly know that they've almost gone. You see, a junk is just a symbol, a talisman, that's all. Hang a painting of a junk on your wall or clip a miniature one onto your keychain, and good fortune is supposed to sail with you. Who knows whether it works or not. Maybe it does. Most people believe so. In one form or another you'll be seeing junks in China for a long time."

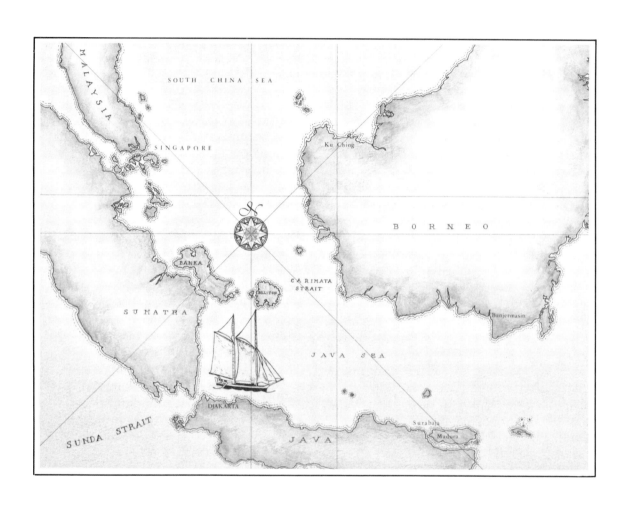

THE INDONESIAN *PINISI*

Beyond the modern port of Jakarta with its orderly concrete quays is another harbor, its historical complement, a dirty, crowded backwater that appears to have been lifted from a Conrad novel. Ringed by a shantytown, the timber port of Kalibaru is always jammed with sailing craft, moored, anchored, rafted, one against the other as though the ships were olives in a jar. There is no system, not even the pretense of order. First come, first served, is the only rule, with the larger boats, schooners of twenty-five and thirty meters, pushing aside the smaller craft. Like animals wiggling toward a feeding trough, the boats arrive and nose their bowsprits toward the shore.

Those forceful or fortunate enough to be no more than a gangplank's distance away unload their cargoes easily. The others, stranded in the labyrinth, off-load their timber plank by plank into small punts that then snake under sterns and bowsprits toward the quay. Should the way be blocked, a half-dozen men push the boats apart and wedge them there with planks. Whenever a boat leaves, there is a noisy scramble for position as everyone shifts his mooring lines and tries to come closer to the shore.

We walked along the muddy quay passing under more than a dozen huge bowsprits, some nearly six meters long. But the windjammer image was deceptive. Most of

the ships, we discovered, rarely use the wind. Their bowsprits are a vestige of the past that has almost ceased to have a function. Much of their running rigging had disappeared, and on most of them a large, blackened exhaust pipe protruded from the deck.

There are still windjammers in Indonesia, hundreds of them, fleets of sail that ply between the islands, but their number is diminishing rapidly, perhaps by as much as fifty percent a year.

At the end of the quay we found a ship with her topmasts still in place. Sails hung limp and drying from her gaff booms and her deck was not blemished by diesel soot. Her name was *The Perfect God*, and she was a *pinisi*, a Buganese schooner of twenty-six meters.

The Bugis are famous for being traders and travelers and also have a long-standing reputation for being rogues, smugglers, and tight-fisted merchants. Although they have colonies in nearly every Indonesian port, their home is in the southern part of the Celebes. Centuries before the Europeans arrived they had a trading empire that covered the entire Malay world.

After the Dutch took control of the archipelago, the Bugis continued to thrive. They adapted rapidly to the new situation, and fit well into the interstices in European trade. They collected small quantities of goods from insignificant and barely ac-

119

cessible ports and delivered them to the *entrepôts* of Batavia and Singapore. They also traded in commodities that the Europeans shunned, like *tripang* (a sea slug), shark's fin, and bird's nest, all Chinese delicacies that still fetch a high price. When the Dutch decreed that spices could be shipped only in Dutch boats, the Bugis quickly became efficient and successful smugglers.

Their boats, the *pinisi*, are dim mirrors reflecting the past, whose structure arises from memory and generations of experience, all tightly bound by tradition. According to legend, the first *pinisi* was built by Sawerigading, a famous Buganese sailor who is thought to have lived in the time of the Ming dynasty. It was he who launched the Buganese into the world of commerce and sent them out to sea to seek their fortunes.

The Buganese still continue to trade, but now only in the outer islands. The majority of the *pinisi*, like *The Perfect God*, are in the timber business, ferrying lumber from Borneo and Sumatra to Java.

We came across a group of sailors sitting on the quay in the shade of the ship's bow.

"Where is she going?" we asked.

"Jambi," one replied.

"No, Palembang," another corrected him.

We climbed on board and talked to the boatswain, who said she was going to Lingga. The cook, who claimed to have seen the agent, was sure she was bound for Benjarmasin.

When we finally found the *juragan*, or captain, ashore in a bar having a breakfast of beer, he shook his head and admitted he hadn't decided what the next port would be. But wherever it was, he said, the boat would sail the following morning with the tide.

As soon as we moved onto *The Perfect God* we met her real owners—cockroaches, thousands of finger-length beasts who sifted through everything on board as though it belonged only to them. The crew was constantly chasing them out of the rice pot and off the sails, often by just gently flicking them aside.

At first, we refused to take such a benign approach. We chased them down, stamped on them, or hurled them overboard while everyone watched bemusedly. It was futile, of course. Fifty or even a hundred cockroaches less made no difference, and we soon accepted them as part of the crew, casually brushing them out of our way. It became an almost unconscious gesture, like scratching mosquito bites. One smoked, or worked, or ate, and occasionally with the other hand whisked the cockroaches aside or slapped the deck to drive the more timid ones temporarily back into the cracks.

At night we pulled our sarongs over ourselves as though they were shrouds and went to sleep. The cockroaches scrambled over everybody. The boat was theirs.

"Don't be too hard on them," the boatswain cautioned. "Save some for later. They make good bait. The fish love them."

The boatswain was older than the captain and had spent more than thirty years sailing through the Indonesian archipelago. Thin and well-muscled, he was still the strongest man on board.

We sat on the foredeck with him and several members of the crew, rolling cigarettes made with spice-scented tobacco and waiting for the captain to appear.

"He's not a very good captain," the

boatswain said. "He doesn't like the boat and we all know it. He's young and never learned much about the sea. He doesn't want to either. He hates it. Whenever we get into trouble he goes into his cabin and won't come out. He sits there and plays with his flashlights. He takes them apart, cleans them, changes the batteries, puts them together, takes them apart again. . . . He goes on like that for hours."

"How did he become a captain?" we asked.

"His family have always been *juragans*, so he became one too. Being a *juragan* is not so bad, you know. You get a lot of money and most of the fun. As soon as we get into port he's the first one to go ashore, off to the women or the bars. He comes back when the money's gone.

"You see, whatever the boat makes on

the cargo gets divided into thirds: one part to the owner, another to the boat, and the third to the crew. After we split up our share among ourselves, each of us doesn't get very much. And don't forget, we have to buy our own food. The captain is the one who does well. He gets ten percent of the owner's share, and it's up to him to decide what to do with the boat's share, whether he wants to buy new ropes or sails or spend it in the bars. He can play around as much as he likes.

"And us? I can tell you what we get—less and less, it seems. Now we're not allowed to have girls on board. That's what the police say. 'No women on the *pinisi!*' The girls come anyway, of course, quietly at night. If the police arrive you have to hide them. But it doesn't do much good. The police always know what you're doing. A bunch of sweating sailors in the middle of the night aren't working, that's for sure. It gets expensive that way. You have to pay the girls and the police too.

"We're not allowed to have cockfights either. I used to keep cocks on board, sometimes as many as twelve of them, and they made me a lot of money too. We'd have fights on the deck and all the sailors came and bet on them. Then a couple of months ago they told us to stop that too. The police came on board and said it was a new law—no more gambling in Indonesia, and if they caught us, we'd go straight to jail. It's a real shame. They were good cocks, all muscle. They were so tough we couldn't eat them."

At about ten o'clock the boatswain went ashore to look for the captain. He was back in only a few minutes. "*Cewek*," he reported, and almost immediately the crew dispersed to go to sleep. Most of them sprawled on the hatch, curled up like puppies, one across the other.

"The captain has gone to the women," the boatswain translated for us.

"When will he come back?"

"Whenever he's finished. Like I said, whenever the money is gone."

The next morning, instead of the captain, the agent arrived with several truckloads of cement and announced we would be sailing for Benjarmasin in Borneo. *The Perfect God* was lucky to have the cargo. Most of the other *pinisi* made the return voyage in ballast.

The loading was a long and tortuous task, literally a feat of endurance. Carrying two sacks at a time, eighty kilos at once, each man climbed up the gangplank, then handed the sacks to another who stood at the hatch. He in turn lowered them halfway down onto a platform, and a third man, the rest of the way. A fourth stacked them neatly in rows.

The air was thick with cement dust. It mixed with the sweat, and dried and caked into an irritating glue. A few tried to protect themselves by wearing plastic bags, but the heat inside them was intense. They worked without rest, hour after hour, each bag of cement passing through four pairs of hands before it found its place in the hold.

We watched the waterline rise. According to her papers, *The Perfect God* was licensed to carry sixty tons of cargo, but she undoubtedly loaded far more than that. The Plimsoll mark dipped into the water, then disappeared altogether.

A port official stood on the quay watching, but took no notice of the overloaded boat. His well-pressed uniform set him

apart from the sailors and stevedores, and from time to time he officiously made notes on his clipboard.

We walked down the gangplank and peered over his shoulder. His interest, he explained, was only in the names and tonnages of the boats arriving and departing. He showed us his records, all neatly lettered in different colors, then invited us to tea in the port office.

A half-dozen other officials were crowded into the small room, stamping and signing manifests or sipping tea, unashamed that their desks were bare. Posters explaining emergency regulations dotted the walls, but it was clear that no one ever enforced them.

All ships, sail or motor, are required to carry a first aid box, for example, but they are never checked. The one on board *The Perfect God* contained two incomplete decks of cards, some dominos, and a miscellany of broken tools.

An accident at sea is treated like an act of God—He has willed it—and it is useless to challenge His omnipotence. Whatever happens has a reason and a purpose and a

The "nails" that hold the hull together are carved from ironwood.

man must accept whatever is dealt to him. Chance and the elements prey upon the Indonesian sailor and in many ways he stands alone before the sea.

"If you enforced all the rules," the official told us, "not one of those *pinisi* would ever leave the harbor. There's not a life raft on any of them. If you ask the captains they'll say they don't need one because the boat can't sink. Maybe not, it's nothing but wood and that's all most of them carry. But they can and do break up. If they hit a rock or a sandbar out there in the middle sooner or later the waves will tear them apart. Then what? Build a raft? They've done that, lashed a bunch of planks together and paddled to shore. Sometimes it takes them days. But not all of them have been so lucky. There's not much we can do about it. They don't have the money to buy life rafts. They never will, and even if they had the money, they'd never buy one. That's the way they think. Rules are made by people who make rules. You can't always expect other people to obey them."

"Are there a lot of accidents?" we asked.

"Yes, of course," he replied, as if surprised we didn't know. "All the time. Nearly every week something happens, maybe serious, maybe not, a wreck, collision, fire. . . . Fires are the worst, and most of them happen right here in port. Look around. Everything you see is made of wood: houses, boats, quay, lumberyards. There's more wood here than in the middle of the jungle, and most of it's dry as tinder. A few sparks and the whole place can go up.

"The fires usually happen at night. No one knows exactly how they get started, but it's easy to guess: some drunk knocks

over a kerosene lamp, or a few coals fall out of a stove that no one is watching. That's enough. A couple of minutes and a house or a boat is aflame. We had three big fires here last year, two of them in the same month. Nearly half the port has been rebuilt." He pointed toward the end of the harbor and we could easily see the extent of the two fires. For fifty or sixty meters along the waterfront the clapboard houses were in various states of construction, while further along a group of new ones all had a reddish color that matched the freshly cut lumber stacked on the quay.

"No one fears fires more than sailors," he went on. "When a fire starts, suddenly it's panic on board the boats. It's terrible. A few flames somewhere, then a couple of minutes later maybe a hundred boats are fighting to get out of the harbor. And everyone knows that not all of them will make it.

"It gets worse every time. More and

more of the sails are made from plastic cloth and when one of those goes up it's almost like an explosion. About a dozen boats were burned in the last fire, and twenty people died, most of them sailors. Some of the lumber ashore burned for days."

The tea arrived and we took it outside. The official gestured toward a group of sailors sitting on a stack of planks and obviously involved in an intense discussion. "You know what they're probably talking about?" he said, "what really makes their hearts flutter? It's not women, or gambling, or smuggling, not anymore. It's engines. They've fallen in love with them. They'll sit there and chatter about them by the hour, how many horsepower, how much it costs, how fast it goes. It's a kind of disease and they're all infected. Engines . . . engines . . . they're the new gods.

"It has a crazy logic to it all. If you own one, no one has to work again. The engine will drive the boat, pump the bilges, hose down the deck, heat the water for tea, and, of course, make lots of money for you. No more sails to hoist or sew. Nothing left to do but lie down under an awning and sleep or watch television while the engine takes you to the next port. As soon as they've got an engine the next thing is a TV set.

"The *pinisi* don't go any faster with an engine—quite the contrary, most of them are slower, often by a couple of knots. They can't afford to buy big engines, so they put in whatever they can get, a truck engine usually. It's probably been rebuilt a half-dozen times before they get their hands on it, so who knows how much power is left. In any case, how fast can a one-hundred-horsepower engine drive a twenty-five-meter boat loaded with one

hundred or more tons of cargo?

"The big advantage is that the boats follow a regular schedule, and that's what the shipping agents like. It doesn't matter how long a voyage takes, if the agent knows in advance what day the boat will arrive. They hate to hold cargoes, or watch some *pinisi* tack back and forth in front of the harbor while the buyers wait for their wood. The agents will get what they want. They always do. After all, they run the trade. In a couple of years every boat here will have an engine. If they don't, they won't get a cargo."

On our second day in port the wind began to pick up. The sky was blue and clear, but soon the rattle of rigging was almost deafening, a clanging staccato that sounded like the prelude to a Chinese opera. It continued into the evening, gathering force and clatter and made sleep almost impossible.

In the middle of the night there was a terrible crash that bounced us awake and upright just in time to watch the gaff boom roll off the coachroof and drop onto the deck. A bit of chain at the crosstrees had worn through and the heavy three-meter spar had come crashing down. Fortunately, everyone was asleep forward, on the deck or the hatch. The crew examined the damage without comment, then left the gaff where it lay and went back to sleep.

After a breakfast of cold rice and soya bean cake the boatswain broke out the ship's stock of tools: a hammer made from a big nut, a well-chipped saw blade, a pair of pliers, and a handful of broken knives. We were short of wire so one of the crew unrolled two strands and joined them, thereby doubling the wire's length and halving its strength.

The temporary lashing we would make would immediately become permanent. Only when something breaks is it repaired, and then as quickly as possible, using whatever might be on hand. If there is no chain, reinforcing rod will be used, if no rod, then wire, if no wire, another length will be unraveled or bits of old rope and strips of sailcloth knotted together. The substitutions are endless and the patchwork almost art. Spars and lines could be checked, of course, from time to time, but then no sailor ever sets out to look for work.

While we sat on the crosstrees maneuvering the gaff into place we noticed a black cloud rising in the direction of Jakarta. Later we went ashore and listened to the radio in a teashop. As usual, the cause of the fire was unknown, and all day the sirens wailed as more and more fire engines headed toward the blaze. Toward evening the smoke gradually dwindled into a wispy plume. Nearly a square kilometer of portside slum had burned to the ground.

The following morning the captain appeared. With difficulty he pulled himself over the bulwarks, surveyed his ship, then wobbled toward the little hut that housed the cookstove. The crew eyed him enviously, knowing they would never to able to afford such a hangover. The captain helped himself to several handfuls of rice, then sat down wearily on the edge of the coachroof.

The most arduous task at sea is manning the cumbersome steering oar, an exhausting battle with wind and waves.

"Let's go. Make sail," he said to the boatswain. Then he lay down, pulled his sarong over his head and went to sleep.

A motorized *pinisi* towed us out a half mile, then we cast off and set all sail: three jibs, two mainsails, and two topsails. Each man had his position, his sail, and his sheets, halyards, and stays. The coordination was amazing. In a matter of minutes, *The Perfect God* began to creak and strain as the wind filled the sails, then she dug deep into the waves and slowly gathered way.

The boatswain consulted the compass, an ancient hand model whose fluid had

Fire is the big danger in the lumber ports, and every few years the port burns and must be rebuilt.

long since drained away, then set the course. It would take us straight into the Indonesian version of the Bermuda Triangle.

A line drawn across the Java Sea from Surabaya in Java to Benjarmasin in Borneo, on to Ujung Pandang (Macassar) in the Celebes forms a triangle that is thought to contain giant fish, phantoms, monsters from the deep, and misty fountains of magic and destruction. The stories are legion: ships that suddenly disappear on calm seas, catch fire during rainstorms, lose their crews, or are attacked by strange beasts.

Superstition and magic are still strong in Indonesia, and for many form an underlying belief system that is overlaid with a Moslem veneer. The sailors we met seldom knelt down for their daily prayers. However, they carefully observed a large number of rituals, taboos, and omens.

Magic can come from anywhere, sky, sea, or land. Sometimes it arrives with the wind and alights on the masthead, sparkling like stars, and signaling that something on board is amiss. Or it can rise from the depths with great brilliance and consume the ship. On shore, stones, especially those near the sea, are often thought to possess magic and many sailors carry one that will protect them in time of need. They rub them occasionally for good luck, and when they are ill the stone is soaked in a glass of water that is later drunk as medicine. Some trees are also magical. A hoop made from the branch of a special tree, cut at a particularly auspicious moment, is said to have saved many sailors. If placed on the sea, fresh water can be drawn from inside the hoop.

Magic can be evil as well. One must be careful what kind of stones are taken on board. One variety is said to get bigger each time you look at it. It grows larger and heavier until eventually it falls through the bottom of the boat and sinks it.

There is also a basic distrust of things that match. Even numbers are to be avoided. The number of planks on the hull must be an odd number, for example, and so must the sections that make up the keel. When loading a *pinisi*, the cargo should not be even with the edge of a plank, nor should spars be laid end to end.

The list of do's and don'ts is so long and so complicated it is easy to violate one inadvertently.

As we put out to sea we sat on the stern,

our feet hanging over the side, and watched Kalibaru shrink in the horizon. The boatswain suddenly ran over to us. "Don't do that," he cried. "Never hang your feet over the side, not when we're leaving port. It's bad luck for the voyage. Who knows what will happen?"

The most treacherous part of the Java Sea Triangle is said to be near the center, the waters that surround the island of Maselembu. Sailors call them "the sea of wandering rocks and islands." More than likely it is not rocks or islands that wander, but underwater sandbanks that shift endlessly with the current. No chart can plot them, and not even the most experienced captain can predict their location. A course that may be safe on one voyage can be dangerous on the next.

We listened to the stories with scepticism. The lore of the sea has always been rich with tales of inexplicable forces and supernatural beings. No one was more surprised than we were when *The Perfect God* became a victim of the Java Sea Triangle.

On the third day out, suddenly and quietly, the motion of the boat ceased. There was no obvious reason. The wind was light. The sails were full. The sea was calm. No land was in sight. Yet clearly we were stopped dead in the water.

The boatswain threw the leadline over the side. The cord went slack almost immediately. *The Perfect God* had gently nosed onto one of the "wandering islands" of sand.

As the boatswain predicted, the captain immediately retreated to his cabin and began to fiddle with his flashlights and batteries.

Without a word the crew broke out some long poles, and two men to a pole, tried to force the ship backward toward deeper water. But she refused to even budge.

We heaved a dugout canoe over the

side, then rowed an anchor fifty meters astern to the edge of the bank. The only route off the sand was the same way we had come on.

A large tree trunk lashed across the bow served as a windlass, and the anchor line was wound around it. The whole crew, twelve men, heaved and strained for an hour without being able to take a single turn on the windlass.

By midday it became too hot to work. The crew lay down in a line in the shade of the mast and fell asleep. We took refuge on a bit of deck in the shade of the deckhouse feeling guilty for having jinxed the voyage.

Our little world of ship and horizon had suddenly become quiet and still. The wind died into an occasional searing puff that barely rippled the blue mirror of sea. *The Perfect God* seemed to be caught in a still life that called to mind a portrait of a windjammer, stranded and desolate in the "Horse Latitudes."

The captain climbed out of his cabin and sat cross-legged on the coachroof watching the sea with obvious disinterest. He had yet to give a single order.

That evening when it was cooler we tried the windlass again, but without success. Every morning and every evening for the next three days we all assembled on the foredeck and groaned and grunted for an hour or so trying to winch the boat free. The rest of the time we slept, or bathed in the sea.

On the morning of the fourth day we awoke to find *The Perfect God* afloat and tugging on her anchor. A high tide had raised the boat by a few inches, just enough for us to be clear of the bar. The tides of the Java Triangle are as unpredictable as the currents. We hauled in the anchor, set sail, and blithely continued on our course.

Almost immediately, the weather turned worse. The clouds thickened and the wind became dangerously moist and cool. A

nasty black line in the sky astern was rapidly overtaking us.

"It's going to be bad," warned the boatswain, "very bad. And soon. Wherever it goes we're going with it."

The black storm face crept across the gentle rollers. On the other side of the rain curtain we could see the growing fury of a wind-whipped sea.

The Perfect God rode so low in the water that her deck was soon awash. Wave after wave rolled over us leaving behind clouds of froth in the scuppers. The first thing to go overboard was the water drum. One wave knocked it over and a second

carried it into the sea. We all raced forward and frantically lashed down what we could—dugout canoe, anchors, lines, and spars, but not before the cook house had gone over the side taking with it our store of rice and the pot.

Water continued to sweep across the boat sending up geysers of spray. The boat rolled heavily out of tune with the wave motion and the deck became a dangerous, unpredictable platform, a little like a carnival ride that makes the most of unexpected movement.

The boatswain took the helm, but it was all he could do just to hold the steering oar

Any stretch of riverbank can become a shipyard.

straight. Even with two men on the oar it couldn't be turned. Why the Bugis have clung to this archaic means of steering is a mystery, especially considering the long contact they have had with the Chinese and Europeans, both of whom use the more efficient center rudder. Stubborn tradition is probably the answer, an unyielding commitment to what is. To change a part is to change the whole. "If she didn't have steering oars," sailors often told us, "she wouldn't be a *pinisi*."

In the storm *The Perfect God* was nearly unmaneuverable. The leeward steering oar was so deep in the water and had so much pressure on it that it couldn't be used, and the windward oar was often in the air. Several times we nearly broached to and the boatswain was powerless to do anything about it. The water swirled about him and he clung to the oar more for balance than for steerage. He fought the storm in his own way, and he seemed to enjoy the struggle, an old man wrestling with the sea.

During a lull between squalls he turned to us and shouted a Chinese proverb: "Once the sails are set and the oar is in place, even if the sails are torn and the oar breaks, you never turn the bowsprit back toward land."

EPILOGUE

The manuscript was finished, our notes filed, and the thousands of slides classified and stored in an archive. But instead of embarking on a new project, we returned to the place where we had started, South America, and began to take a second look at "the last sailors." However, this time we carried movie cameras, and there were more of us as well.

The idea of making a documentary film began shortly after we had started work on the book. We quickly realized that our subject was far more extensive than we had thought. The numerous remnants of working sail scattered around the world are but the tip of an iceberg, vestiges of a maritime culture that once flourished on nearly every navigable river and along every hospitable coast. We wanted to create a visual, humanistic document, something that would reflect not only the present, but the past as well. We set out to make the film with the same spirit with which we made the book—letting working sailors act and speak for themselves.

Fortunately, working sail is inherently photogenic. Men, sails, and water are dramatic in almost any combination, and in any weather, but especially so when the sailors set out to struggle with the elements to earn their livelihood at sea.

To make the film we needed a professional crew, and a substantial sum of money, several digits more than we possessed. All the little items on the budget, and a few big ones like travel and film stock, added up to a very large total. As is the case with most films, locating funds became the major problem. It was pointless to begin before all the money was committed.

In Paris we met Rob Maclean, a young Canadian film producer who was also a sailor. He had heard about our project from a mutual friend at a cocktail party. Names were exchanged and when we arrived back from Egypt a telegram was waiting for us: "Please call me immediately. Urgent. Any time."

We met in an old café near the canal St. Martin, a dingy bistro full of bargemen and dockers, where two years before we had first discussed the possibility of writing a book about working sail. After a few rounds of Calvados we took out a plastic sheet of slides and held them to the light against a frosted glass partition.

Rob looked at them carefully—a dozen sea-weary boats, and a dozen weathered faces who would not have been out of place at the bar beside us.

"When were they taken?" Rob asked.

"This year."

He studied the pictures once again. "Can you find them again if we go back to film?"

"Most of them," we replied.

"It will make a fantastic documentary,"

he said. "I'll find the money. And . . . I'm coming with you."

He did both.

For Rob, filmmaking is a simple and straightforward process, and when it becomes otherwise—which, unfortunately, it often does—he becomes determined that the circumstances fit his perspective. With unlimited bursts of energy he wrestles with a problem until he reduces it to a manageable form he can conquer. And from the moment we shook hands in the café until we looked at the first print of the film in Montreal nearly two years later, there was never a shortage of problems.

Once the project was funded we began to look for a cameraman who was accustomed to working under adverse conditions. He had to be a sailor, someone who could film from the masthead without getting seasick, and he had to be willing to take a chance to get an exceptional shot. The combination was not easy to find. It is one thing to sit in an air-conditioned bar and discuss the techniques of filming sailboats, and quite another to live the hardships of the working sailor and film them from his point of view.

After several trials—and several errors—we found two cameramen who were able to cope with the difficult conditions: Ron Precious, a veteran of many Greenpeace victories at sea, and John Cressey, who had made films for UNESCO in the underdeveloped world.

Cressey filmed most of the series. A genial, sardonic Canadian, he proved to be a chameleon, capable of fitting into almost any setting, and, when necessary, vanishing into a crowd. Instead of concealing his camera, as one might be tempted to do,

John did precisely the opposite. He was obvious and obtrusive, and poked his lens wherever the inquiring eye would go. The camera was always on his shoulder, and he studied his subject constantly. Eventually man and camera would blend into the location. We developed an elaborate set of codes so that no one else knew when the film was running.

For sailors in search of a film, the logistics were prodigious. We planned to make five offshore voyages, travel down three major rivers, and film in the ports and along the coasts of fourteen countries, all of them in the Third and Fourth World, and most of them extremely sensitive about their image abroad. The volume of paperwork was enormous. Suddenly, wherever we went we were secretaries instead of sailors, engulfed by a sea of correspondence. We established a company—Adventure Film Productions—and our office became a suitcase filled with records and stationery.

It was one thing for two of us to travel with a couple of Leicas concealed in a dirty canvas bag, and quite another to arrive in an airport or harbor with a film team, cameras and sound equipment, cases of film, and tripods. No matter how light and unobtrusive we tried to be, the sheer volume of the gear was enough to attract attention. Customs inspectors and police pounced on us like pirates on a galleon.

Our only defense was a barrage of letters, documents, equipment lists, and certifications, all of them stamped, sealed, initialed, and photocopied. Wherever we went, we left behind a wake of paper.

More than once some heavily epauletted officer took us aside and studied us and our baggage carefully. His look voiced the unasked question, "What are they really here to do?" We could almost hear him think, "An American, a German, and a couple of Canadians, bearded and carrying passports full of stamps, are telling me they have come all this way just to film sailboats. Why? Who are they?"

There were, of course, several possibilities that occurred to him—intelligence agents seeking to photograph naval installations, drug smugglers collecting a shipment, arms dealers peddling weapons to some dissident sect or faction, or even white slavers looking for women to stock brothels in the Middle East.

At one time or another we were accused of being all of them. We joked and reasoned and argued and discovered that proving what you are not is often far more difficult than proving what you are.

In most countries an official was assigned to us, a guide and a watchdog, to help us should we actually be making a film, and to keep track of us if we were not.

Their suspicions often outweighed their usefulness, and we were constantly amazed at their abilities to twist fact into fantasy. Going out late at night to buy a pack of cigarettes could be translated into an act of conspiracy, or collecting mail at an embassy into a clandestine meeting to drop off microfilm. There were no limits.

One Asian chaperone became convinced we were drug dealers, and the more we protested, the more he believed we were lying. According to him, we went to sea every day not to film, but to look for a shipment left on a buoy by a freighter. He followed us everywhere, waiting for money to change hands, and hoping, obviously, to get a piece of the action for himself. When the pick-up at sea failed to take place, he reasoned that, in fact, it had—he had only failed to catch us. Certain that we had the drugs, he offered—for a small fee, of course—to help us past customs at the airport. We refused, and as a consequence were thoroughly searched, but to no effect. Just before we boarded the plane our guide took us aside and congratulated us. "I don't know how you did it," he said, "but it's good to work with professionals." Then he handed us a small packet. "Next time buy from me. I've got the best in the country."

On another occasion in Sri Lanka we found ourselves at the mercy of a shipping agent who was also the "godfather" of the port. A good word from him and we could sail and film immediately. Without his consent no captain would dare take us on board.

The agent invited us to dinner and during the meal he questioned us as though filling in forms. The moment he discovered we were single, the interview suddenly became focused and we learned that our shipping agent was also a marriage broker.

He excused himself from the table and returned a few minutes later to announce that we would be having lunch the next day with several eligible ladies, all from good families and with European educations. "Don't worry," he announced. "I told them you were sailors. So they know what to expect."

We were caught. If the meeting went well, he certainly wouldn't let us sail. If it went badly, he wouldn't let us leave either. The time had come for one of us to fall in love. We drew straws.

The lunch turned out to be excellent, and the ladies were certainly as charming as he said they were. One of them was so charming, in fact, that one of us elected to stay behind. The agent was delighted, and the rest of the crew sailed with the next tide.

To make the film we went to most of the same locations we used for this book, and we followed the same route. We began in South America and slowly worked our way eastward, retracing our steps. It was an unusual opportunity to see what changes had occurred in each of the sailing communities during our absence, and we wanted to make the most of it. Hence, we tried to film the same "last sailors" who appear in this book, so that book and film would fuse into a single document.

We returned to the south of Chile and discovered a dramatic change. The raw, sleepy, frontier atmosphere was gone. Despite the country's many economic problems money was now flowing southward to develop the vast resources in the southern Andes. Life in Puerto Montt had turned the century and was rapidly striding toward the present.

Every country has its own "moon project," a nearly impossible dream that takes years, if not decades, to realize. For Chile, it is a road, a three-thousand-mile highway that will eventually span the country from north to south, from Peru to the Tierra del Fuego.

Bulldozers have already begun work on the stretch that will connect Puerto Montt with Chiloe continental, and when it is completed, the *lanchas chilotas* will be competing with huge logging trucks, a struggle that will not last for long.

We sailed from Puerto Montt on board the *Trauco,* a *lancha* that had been remade into a yacht. A Santiago banker had graciously loaned her to us, and as soon as we cleared the harbor we pointed her bow southward toward the fjord where Osvaldo has his farm.

We arrived in the early morning and dropped anchor beside his *lancha chilota.* Once again the smell of freshly baked bread wafted across the water, and we were soon seated around the stove juggling hot biscuits.

But Osvaldo was not there. He had found a job with the roadbuilders, and for months at a time he was deep in the mountains cutting trails through the virgin forest. His wife told us most families have a man or two working on the road.

Osvaldo's son was now captain of the *lancha,* but his dreams were clearly elsewhere—behind the wheel of a logging truck or in the *cantinas* of Puerto Montt. For him, sea and sail mean a life of solitude, a prison where he endlessly hauls wood from the forest to the market.

"Soon my father will let me work on the road," he told us proudly, "then we'll sell the *lancha* for firewood."

He sailed with us to Rio Negro, welcoming the excuse to leave the farm.

Wherever we stopped we asked about Lucia, the used-clothing merchant who had bought a share of a motor launch. She was an unusual woman, an exception in macho-land, who had managed to stand alone. Everyone knew her, but not where she was. She had "gone south" with her boat, we were told, down to the thousands of islands that are still beyond the frontier. We learned that many people have "gone south," and apparently every new extension of the road sends another small wave of immigrants deeper into the wilderness where they will have a little longer to wait before the first bulldozer arrives.

Jody de Silva, the Brazilian community development officer who had worked with the *jangadieros,* met us at the airport. He had been transferred to the slums, where he was trying to help migrant laborers cope with urban life—"the same impossible task," he called it. The government had curtailed assistance to the fishing villages as part of an austerity program and the *jangadieros* were left to fend or fail for themselves.

Jody drove us to the village where we had stayed the last time and we looked for Roberto, the fisherman with whom we had lived and sailed. The meeting was an unexpected shock, a few awkward moments while we realized what had happened in our absence. Roberto stood motionless in the doorway of his hut, leaning on a crutch, one leg withered and twisted into an unnatural position.

Not long after we left, he explained, his *jangada* had turned over in the surf. Everyone else was thrown clear, but he had been caught underneath the raft and his leg broken in several places. The bones had been badly set, and he was left a cripple, condemned to the shore where he was unable to earn a living. His children had been sent to live with relatives. He and his wife now lived alone.

He had found a job as custodian of the village well, but it was more charity than work and he knew it. Every morning at dawn he hobbled to the windmill and unlocked the pump. Then he sat and smoked for an hour while the women drew their water. Even with a crutch Roberto moved gracefully, maintaining his dignity, but it was clear that his vitality was gone.

One stormy afternoon while we were filming from the beach a *jangada* slipped off the front of a wave and pitch-poled. The crew was lucky. They were washed ashore by the next wave and came out of the surf unharmed.

The *jangada* floated in behind them. Even the day's catch was saved.

Roberto turned and quietly hobbled away, hiding his envy and his grief.

In Cairo, we returned to Issa's hay market, where our cameras had a commanding view of the waterfront.

Issa was unchanged—placid and inscrutable. He still had eight *aiyassas* that hauled hay to his market, and the same one we traveled on the year before was tied up at the quay.

In the afternoon the *rais,* or captain, came ashore to take tea with Issa under a huge awning. As is the custom, Issa presides over his little court of captains, sailors, laborers, and anyone else who happens by and is in need of shade.

"Trade is still bad," he began, setting the theme that he would embroider with infinite patience. Issa enjoyed his complaints. They were always good social currency, subjects that would never wear out.

Several other captains joined the group, and when Issa finished, our *rais* began telling yarns about our last voyage—how we broke an anchor, fouled lines, gybed the boat, and generally behaved like landlubbers while we struggled to learn how to sail an *aiyassa*. Unfortunately, most of the tales were true. Before the laughter subsided from one story, the *rais* began another.

Finally he stood up, embraced us both,

then took our tripod and planted it firmly on the bows of his *aiyassa,* letting everyone know that despite our faults and foibles he would sail with us again.

We arrived in Sri Lanka and discovered that working sail is disappearing quickly. As our taxi passed the harbor at Negumbo we made a rough count of the *oruwas*— half the number that had been there the year before. Several hulks lay drawn up on the beach, weathered wrecks that were playthings for children, and a small quay had replaced part of the *oruwa* anchorage. The lagoon was lined with small motorboats, the traditional smell of dried fish now laced with diesel fumes.

Despite the modern tide, Stanley still had his *oruwa,* and what's more, he had prospered. Tourism was growing in Sri Lanka. The beach hotels were filled with sun-seeking Europeans and it seemed like every one of them wanted a prawn cocktail for dinner. Buyers from the resorts had taken over the prawn market, and their appetites were insatiable. Whatever Stanley and his crew could catch was sold immediately.

Stanley welcomed us like long-lost shipmates. There was now one more child in his family, and one more room in his house, a new brick kitchen he had built himself. The walls were papered with postcards we had sent him, each one encased in a painted cardboard border—the art in the frame, not in the picture.

We crowded into the new kitchen, and Stanley proudly served us the finest coconut arrak, illicit white lightning guaranteed to wreck any sailor. Whatever had been planned for later that day was immediately canceled. With brimming glasses we toasted Stanley's good fortune.

Unfortunately, the profits will not last forever. At best, his *oruwa* will be usable for another four or five years, then it will be too waterlogged to go to sea. The current ban on lumbering has been effective, and Stanley will be unable to find new logs to rebuild his boat.

But he was not concerned about the future, nor was he envious of the motorboats that were gradually replacing the *oruwa* fleet. He ignored them and virtually everything else tainted with modernity. Somehow, he could accept us and all our complicated equipment with open arms, but he could not accept innovation for himself. His perspective was parochial and consistent, a traditional formula that had always worked in the past. The *oruwa* fisherman lives in the present, with whatever he possesses at the moment. Money on hand is to be spent; fish to be eaten. His problems are contained in today. Tomorrow he can go fishing again.

We lashed a movie camera to the outrigger, and followed the *oruwa* fleet through the surf. For several days we fished with Stanley, often trawling for prawns within sight of the hotels where they would be eaten.

A new form of *oruwa* fished alongside us, identical in form, but made from fiberglass, its hull bright and glistening. Only the struts and masts were wooden. The rest of the boat had been fabricated with space-age materials.

Stanley saw the new *oruwa* for what it was, a slick substitute designed to seduce fishermen into trading tradition for expediency. "It's not an *oruwa,*" he told us several times, "it's a plastic pail, and I'm not going to sea in one."

In Bangladesh we were politely informed that since the military had taken over the country it would be "wise to ignore" the contacts we had made on our last visit. A new army of officials was waiting to battle with our paperwork, and they would help us find the men and ships we needed.

The warning was unnecessary.

It was nearly impossible to find most of the sailors we had met on our previous trip. Searching for the captain of the *shampan* on which we sailed would be like looking for a friend "somewhere" in New York City. There are so many serpentine avenues and alleys in the delta that meeting him was almost a statistical impossibility. Yet, whenever we were on the river we looked for the familiar pattern of his sails. Unfortunately, we never saw them.

The doctor on the island of Kutubdia had been transferred to another remote part of the country—banishment, we were told, for having supported the wrong faction in the struggle for power.

The one sailor we did find was the man who had fought the pirates along the Burmese coast. He was in the same tea shop where he had left him, at the same table, and undoubtedly he was telling the same stories. Another veteran had joined him, and his fresh wounds testified to the fact that the pirates are still there.

The first time we were in Macau we had sailed with the Portuguese Marine Police and had accompanied them on patrols along the edges of their tiny enclave. Chinese sailing junks plying the coast often sail through Portuguese waters and we had photographed them easily. Once again the Marine Police took us out on patrol, our tripod tied to the gun on the foredeck.

From the Macanese sailors on board we learned that the stream of boat people from Vietnam is continuing, not with the same intensity as before, but no week passes without the arrival of another small flotilla of refugees.

As fewer and fewer motorboats are available, the number of sailing craft making the journey is increasing—old junks, and occasionally even reed basket boats rigged with makeshift sails. It is perhaps the last mass migration that will take place under sail.

The captains we spoke to when we had visited the refugee camps the year before had all been sent to new homes, most to the United States, where they now sail in modern trawlers. A new group of sailors has replaced them, and, if anything, their accounts of endurance and privation are more astounding. Vietnamese naval patrols have become more efficient and brutal, and the pirates have become better armed. Aside from the human suffering, these men have managed to sail boats full of landlubbers, with only a few inches of freeboard, past a blockade and across hundreds of miles of open water, often without even a compass. Their stories document some of the most incredible small boat voyages ever made.

In Jakarta a port official had kept a log of sail for us—the number of sailing craft that arrived and departed in the past year. He plotted the statistics, and at a glance we could see the decline of the trading schooner: the number of sailings in December were half what they had been in January.

However, the waterfront still maintains a nineteenth-century look. Every craft has masts and yards and a long bowsprit nosed ashore. But in the hold is a diesel engine, and the men on board would rather be mechanics than sailors.

In Surabaya we found *The Perfect God,* the schooner that had taken us to Borneo the year before. She was tied up at the quay, unloading lumber.

She had a new captain, but the old boatswain was still in charge of the crew. That evening we had dinner on board, and after the captain left the boatswain passed out spice-scented cigarettes and then told us what had happened to the old one.

One night during the monsoon he had come back from his rounds probably a little more drunk than usual. It was raining hard and the crew was asleep aft under a tarpaulin. The captain slipped on the gangway and fell in the water. If he screamed or shouted, no one heard him. He drowned there—in port, between the quay and his ship.

"The new captain is no better," the boatswain added. "And it's not his fault. It's hers." He brought his fist down hard on the deck. "There's something wrong with this ship that can never be cured. I didn't tell you about it before, but that's why we got caught by the 'wandering sands.' The seas don't like her. On the next trip they want to put in an engine, and cut down one mast, but it won't make any difference. She'll kill men until she dies herself."

The Last Sailors is now a two-and-a-half-hour film narrated by Orson Welles, a document that cannot be remade. The world of working sail is shrinking rapidly. Every day sails come down that will never be hoisted aloft again. *The Last Sailors* is a summary of that world, a short epitaph for one of man's oldest means of transport.